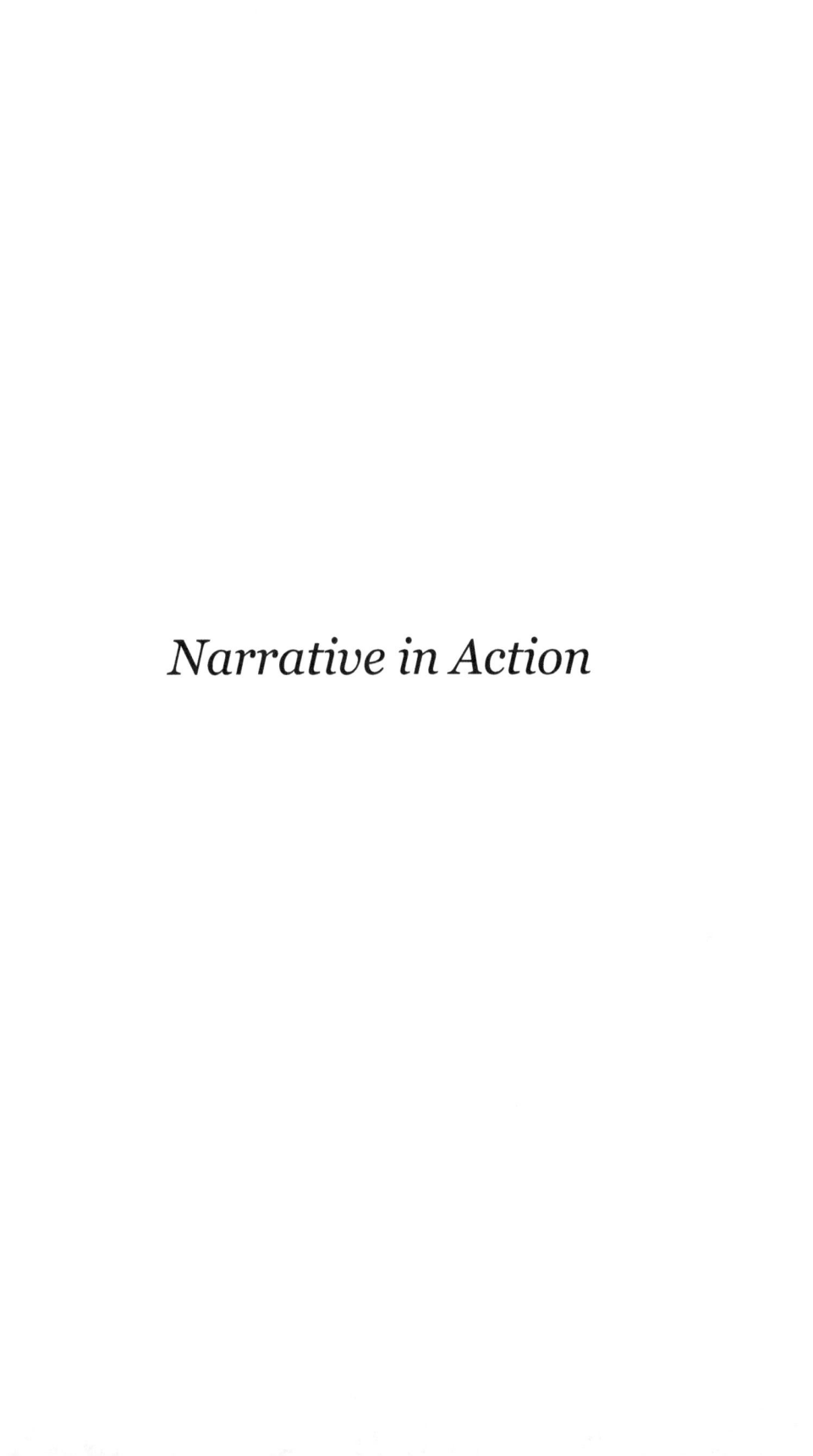

Narrative in Action

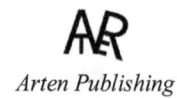

Arten Publishing

In memory of Dave Browning, one of the greatest teachers I've ever known.

Introduction

What's the greatest story ever told?

You might be tempted to pick your favorite film, TV show, book, short story, video game, or perhaps even a song (or even other types of media) in response to this question. Good. Throughout this book, in fact, I want you to keep in mind what your favorite stories are, in whatever form they take, and ask yourself why these stories appeal to you, what about them draws you into their world, makes you care about their characters, makes you keep watching, go to the next episode, turn the page, or continue playing the game. *Why do you care?*

Caring for something is a trait older than humans ourselves; I'd argue, in fact, that apathy, the lack of this trait, is one of the greatest dangers in the world. Passion and compassion are two of the greatest tools that humans have to fight apathy, and stories are one of the ways in which we engage with both of them. So, whether you're a born storyteller or just love stories, keep your interest up. What I hope to do with this book is help you more fully appreciate the art of stories, of how they interface with our world, and of their continued – and, I'd argue, permanent – importance to human society. And if you are a storyteller, I hope to help deepen your understanding of stories, as well.

Before I provide you with my answer to the question of the greatest story ever told, I think it's important to define what a story is, so that you and I are on the same page. This may at first seem pretty condescending; I mean, you've told and experienced stories since you were a little kid, and it might seem as if I'm treating you like one by saying this. However, when something is as ubiquitous a concept as "story," we can easily forget all of its implications. After all, there's such a wide difference between 2019's *Avengers: Endgame* and the events which drive your everyday life that we might forget that both of these fall under the massive category of "story." So, for now, we can define a story (also known as "narrative") as "a sequence of intentionally-collected actions and/or events which cohere together to convey an experience through a medium to a receiver."

Okay, so I apologize for getting a little academic here, but I need to be broad in order to define what a story is. What I mean by a "medium" is the method through which a story is transmitted. For instance, if I tell my friend the story of how I ran into an acquaintance of ours at a restaurant, the medium is the spoken word, whereas if I wrote that story in a journal it would be in a written medium, and if I filmed a re-creation of the encounter, it would be in a visual medium.

Of course, these boundaries aren't strict, as evidenced by, for example, comics, which combine the written and the visual, and comics can be called a medium. What makes a medium, then, is that it uses features distinct to itself to communicate a message. The person who receives this message is therefore called a *receiver*. In an age of technological complexity, the already-blurrable boundaries between media become even more blurred, to the point where it isn't clear what constitutes a specific medium. Is YouTube a distinct medium in and of itself? We'll deal with this in a future chapter, but for now, make your own determination based on what you know and what we've already discussed.

Also, when I say "intentionally-collected," all I mean is that the series of actions and/or events is put into a medium by someone; as opposed to events in the real world, which just happen, stories are collected by someone into a medium in order to transmit the story to another person, and that person does so intentionally.

So, using this definition, it becomes clear that stories are all around us, which may perhaps be obvious. Which one of these is my answer to the question of what is the greatest story ever told? Well, maybe you already know where I'm going with this, but here goes: History. The story of how humanity has interacted with this world and with each other.

History is in a sense the ultimate story. Whether personal or global, it is the root of all inspiration for the fictional stories we tell in every medium. Life is stranger than fiction, apparently, but on top of that, true inspiration is impossible. We interact with the world, absorbing information and responding to it even before we're born, the first cries of a newborn their audible response to a new world, as one no longer umbilically attached to another. So, as a sidenote, if you wish to create, do not shun inspiration from the world because it makes you unoriginal; in fact, embrace your inspirations, whatever they are. Use them to help construct your own narratives, or respond to the work with your own, in whatever medium you work.

However, history is *not* the past. What? Well, yeah, history isn't the past. The past is merely what has happened before the present. Rather, history is a *record* of the past. When speaking about the history of humans collectively, the stories of trade, national conflicts, power exchange, etc., what we know is what has come down to us, put into a convenient series of events in hindsight. This helps us see the interrelated developments of our ancestors' past, but history can never be the past, nor can it truly represent the past.

If it did, it would be like a story (see how often that word pops up in this book) I once heard. A king wished for a grand map of his kingdom, and as it became more and more detailed, it grew and grew until it was as large as the kingdom itself. Not only do I consider this the prime parable of the study of media itself, but I also see in this the tug-of-war between history-as-accurate-representation and history-as-condensation. History helps us make sense of our societies' pasts and learn lessons for their futures. We learn about history, the thinking goes, so that it doesn't repeat itself, so that we progress over time.

This form of history, what I called global, isn't the only form, though. There is also the personal history. Stories we tell our friends and family about our own experiences, as well as the narratives each and every single one of us carves out in our journey from those aforementioned first breaths to our last; a series of events transmitted through a medium (our bodies) to a receiver (our memory). Like history, however, our memory doesn't possess every detail of everything we've ever experienced (with a possible exception of those with eidetic memory, though that's irrelevant for our purposes here, in this book). Our brains condense information in memories and then use them as those building blocks of a narrative. In this process, the memories of the past inform present actions, which in turn create more memories upon which we can build in the future, in a cycle which theoretically continues our personal progress. Action, reaction, cause and effect, another important component of narratives.

This phenomenon is present in all stories, including this very book, which is a condensation of an uncountable number of thoughts down to coherent sentences which are delivered in a logical sequence through the written medium to provide you, the reader, with ideas. So, this book is also an interpretation of reality itself, and it therefore cannot do everything. This is what I also want to point out in this book, that you are not passive in this process.

Meaning is not created in this book, made up of little scribbles on a page; rather, meaning is created by an interplay between you and me, in the interaction that this book facilitates. I can't see you, and you can't see me, but we're communicating. I'm taking thoughts from my brain and putting them into the medium of the written word, and you are taking those written words into your brain and deciphering meaning from them. *You* are a co-creator of meaning.

This goes for the spoken word, as well, where what you hear people say would just be sounds exported to the ether if you weren't there to give meaning to them. In other words, if a tree falls in the forest on top of someone and no one is around to hear their cries for help, do their words still have meaning?

Even visual information is like this, with images in reality or transmitted through a screen being merely flashes of light until they land on our retinas and we can discern meaning from them. It's just, this is more universal, being cross-linguistic and even cross-species, as all animals with visual perception engage in this same process. Written language, and the complexity of spoken and signed language, is only in use by humans.

Beyond this truth about meaning-making, however, I ask that you don't just take in everything I say and accept it as absolute truth, or the end of the story. Think about everything I tell you, and ask yourself if you'd give this point or that point validity or you'd push back on it and say "No, I actually think things work this way, and here's why." That is a wonderful exercise, and human knowledge progresses not by isolated genius (and I'm in no way a genius, just a guy who likes stories), but by collaboration, between individuals across space and time. This is a beauty of the human experience. Also, along that line, don't assume what's in here is the end of the story, no pun intended. Take what I've given you and go further with it. Refine it for your own needs, for instance, or think about how it could be taken further, or improved. This book is all for you.

––––––––

So, before we get into the book itself, I want to end this introduction with a discussion of why I'm writing this whole thing. Why, out of all the things I could be doing, am I engaging in this activity? In fact, who am I, besides a person purporting to have knowledge of the storytelling process? I'm going to answer both of these questions in one go.

My story of how I came to be here, putting this book together, starts on the rainy Monday morning of February 18, 2008. At the time, I was ten years old, and was off from school because it was Presidents Day. My dad came into the room that morning to wake me up. My bed was by the far wall, across from a desk I had moved into my room from our guest room recently. Well, "desk" is a generous term; it was, in reality, our old kitchen table, one we'd stored up in the guest room for many years. The old kitchen chair – with the soft seat but a wooden, mostly-open back, four legs, and no arm-rests – gave away the origin of this piece of furniture, and its original purpose. But I didn't care; a desk made me feel official and grown-up, even if it would take another eight years before I was legally an adult.

The rain presented a problem, because my normal response would've been to go outside and play, since it was still at a point where technology wasn't everything to us at that age. Almost none of us ten-year-olds had phones, and the ones who did all had flip phones, which wouldn't have provided much in the way of entertainment. We had TVs, sure, and those were always a viable option, but streaming services weren't a thing in most of our houses. DVRs, which now seem like a thing of the distant past, were the big thing for that, but I wasn't feeling like TV. My family had to share a single computer at that point, too, so it maybe it was occupied.

So, if I wasn't going outside, what was I going to do? Well, the day before I'd bought a green composition book, spiral-bound, and it was still sitting on that aforementioned desk, waiting for me. I decided that today, I was going to sit down and write.

I went over to the desk and sat down. I grabbed a pencil from my cup of writing instruments (a mug with "VIP DAD" written on it, one I'd borrowed from downstairs), opened to the first page, and stared at it. It seemed so full of potential, so inviting, yet also so broad. Could I really do this, write a story like the ones I read in class? What would I write about?

The answer to my question came in the form of what was then my favorite film, *National Treasure: Book of Secrets*. I'd seen the film in the past month or so in theaters, and I was floored by it. I loved the characters, and both the charisma and the intelligence which seemed to exude from Nicolas Cage's character, Ben Gates. I loved the musical score, which was executed brilliantly by Trevor Rabin, an opinion which I still stand by. I loved the historical components, so much so that it ignited a love of history which has never left me, and helped get me to finally start succeeding as a student in school. For that final reason, I owe this movie – one which I admit now isn't the best, and is pretty cheesy, but it will forever have a pass in my mind – an incredible debt. Well, I actually owe it two, since it's also the reason I started writing. It's the reason I bought the green spiral notebook.

The story I wrote over the next day or two only took up two and a half pages of that notebook, but when I finished it, I was incredibly proud of what I'd created. Titled "British Treasure," the story followed four friends, led by a character named Ray (taken as an anagram for the name "Ryan," minus the "n"), who looked for a treasure and followed a clue to find it. It's absolutely terrible, but I love it, because it shows the passion of a ten-year-old to create something new, something meaningful. I wrote four more stories in the series, each of which were about two pages long in the notebook, but they were all created out of that same desire.

Over the next many years, I would try my hand at writing detective fiction, science fiction, and screenplays. Screenwriting got me interested in filmmaking, an interest which completely changed the course of my life thanks to the college I went to, and the activities and classes I took while attending college. This book wouldn't be here without all of that.

So, why am I writing this? Because of the love I have for this craft of telling stories, regardless of the medium in which the story is told.

That's all well and good, but why am I qualified to write this? The short answer is, I don't know that I am. I may sound like I have no confidence in myself, but that isn't it. Life is a learning process, and you never stop learning new things about the world, and about yourself. Every day I fall in love again with telling stories (my main medium is writing, but that definitely isn't the only one), and I know that I'll do this until the day I die (whenever that is) and I'll do it regardless of whether or not I get paid (though that doesn't mean I'll work for free). Because it's not about the money or about the validation of fame and/or acclaim; it's about something *more*, like I said, some amorphous ideal I can't adequately describe but which I can definitely feel. I believe that we all can feel it, and I also believe, like I said, that stories connect us all.

So, this book will be a learning process for me, as well; in codifying ideas, solidifying disparate thoughts regarding this craft, and analyzing processes, I expect to learn, too. Socrates was the wisest man in Athens because he alone knew that he knew nothing. In life, sometimes our recognition and acceptance of our limitations and what we don't know is just as important as knowing what we do know. To know one's own lack of knowledge is to know what one must learn. So, I hope you'll accompany me on this journey, and that you learn some things along the way, too.

Optional Exercise: Journaling

As a recommendation, I suggest an exercise of a very common sort: keep a journal. This is a chronicle of your personal history at the present moment. Keep it for as long of a timespan as you wish, and in whatever form you wish, but I recommend making an entry at least once a week, to develop a habit. Keeping a journal is good writing practice (if you choose to incorporate writing into your journal in some way), is a good way to deal with daily experiences, and, as I said before, is a record of your life. You will begin to intuit some good narrative practices by merely reciting what happened in your day and how you reacted to it.

Part 1: Narrative Analysis

Chapter 1: The Basics of a Story

It might seem like the introduction was the beginning of things for this book, and that it already covered the basics, but the point of that introduction was really to do just that, introduce. It was meant to introduce *the book*, as opposed to the concepts; the only real concept from it that you need going forward is the definition of story, which we're going to work with. I'll restate our definition of story here: "a sequence of intentionally-collected actions and/or events which cohere together to convey an experience through a medium to a receiver." We're going to work with this definition for the rest of the book, so keep it at the forefront of your mind.

Okay, so we now have a definition for what a story is, and we know that a *medium* is a form of communication and a *receiver* is the person who gets the message. That's all well and good, but what do we define as an action or an event? Can we actually apply this to a real story to see if it works? Well, yes! The following will be our example:

The last person on Earth heard a knock at the door.

So, this gem, according to the friend who told me this, is the world's shortest horror story. But, as you know, we're not here to take things at face value. So, is it what my friend said it was?

Leaving aside the question of whether or not this is a horror story (which is a question of genre, something we'll deal with in a subsequent chapter), is this a *story*? Well, it is communicated through a medium to a receiver. For me, the medium was the spoken word; for you, it's the written one, but so far so good. But what about the first part of our definition, the series of actions which cohere to convey the experience? Does it fit that?

"Wait!" I hear you say, "you defined medium and receiver, but you didn't define what an action or event was." Fair enough. Let's define what those terms are, because they're not interchangeable, but they serve the same purpose.

What do you think of when you hear or see the word "action"? My guess is that you think of someone doing something. Running? Bathing? Sleeping? An **action** doesn't have to be active, it just has to be "something that an agent *does*." (By "agent," I simply mean the thing that does the action; it doesn't have to be a person.)

What do you think of when you hear or see "event"? A trip? A birthday? A party? All of these are events, but that's how we often use the term in real life, in everyday speech. For our purposes, we can define an **event** as "something that happens to someone." Whereas with an action a person (or thing) is doing something, in an event something is being done to them. Actions and events can in many instances be the same thing *except* for being viewed from the opposite frame of reference. It's like saying "Ryan wrote the book" versus "The book was written by Ryan." They mean the same thing, but the subject of the sentence is different. The first sentence is told in the active voice, while the second sentence is told in the passive voice. Something is being done to the subject in the passive voice.

This is why teachers often vehemently push students away from the passive voice, because it's literally *weak*. The subject isn't doing anything. It may seem like a dumb distinction with the example I gave you, so how about we use something where the action is a bit more consequential? Let's try this: "Luke lunged with his lightsaber at the Emperor" versus "the Emperor was lunged at by Luke with his lightsaber."

You can see why the passive voice is often awkward in writing (and, in that sentence, confusing, since it isn't clear whose lightsaber it is). Just as the passive voice is awkward, so is a passive character, one who is carried along the river of plot without having any agency. However, in real life, people don't always have agency with everything. A story with all actions and no events can be boring (there's no challenge to the protagonist), but a story with all events and no actions is also boring (because the protagonist doesn't do anything). Therefore, the ideal when creating a *good* story is a good balance between these two.

So, after that very long-winded answer, let's look back at our example. Does this apply? Do we have a story, based on our definition? Yes! Now, before I tell you why it fits, you can take a moment to see if you can formulate a reason why, before you read the next section, where I break down everything and explain why it's a story.

———

We have a subject, "The last person on Earth" (whom I'll henceforth call "Elpy," because of the initials, "LP"). Good. The story is being told from their perspective, therefore we have a protagonist. (Keep in mind, "protagonist" does not mean "hero." In a story told from the point of view of the Batman villain the Joker, the Joker is the protagonist, and Batman the antagonist. Often, the protagonist is the hero, but not always. "Hero or villain?" is a moral judgment, while "protagonist or antagonist?" is about the perspective from which the story is being told. An antagonist is the force of opposition for the protagonist. That's it.)

Second, we have our protagonist, Elpy, performing an action, "heard."

But what did they hear? "A knock at the door." Yay, an event! That also gives us an implied antagonist (IA, hence "Ayeay"), because *something* has to knock at the door. Maybe it's just something that fell over due to the wind, but the story doesn't give any indication for that, so the assumption, based on the story, is that something, whatever it was, *intentionally* knocked on the door.

Now, wait a minute: (1) isn't "heard" a passive action? (2) Am I not just separating these into two things when they're really one, since there's only one verb in the sentence-story?

(1) "Passive" doesn't always mean that someone is literally a passive character. To say "John received a package" is still an active sentence (though not a story), since John is doing something, namely *receiving* a package. Sure, maybe hearing isn't a very interesting action on its own, but we're not making a judgment about the quality of this one-sentence story; our focus here is on structure.

(2) Just like Ayeay is implied, so too is the second component. "Knock" is a noun in this sentence, but it tells us that something knocked. Because the story is told from the perspective of Elpy, anything Elpy does is an action, and anything Ayeay does is an event, because it's being done to Elpy, though in this case it's being done in an indirect way.

Since there are two things that happen, we have a sequence, and the events cohere, so we thus have a story. Awesome, we now have a starting example, and are beginning to understand what makes a story a story. Some of the components are implied through the story and not explicitly shown, but they're there because of how the story is constructed. Your mind fills in those gaps through those implications, the same way your mind fills in the action between the panels of comics, or thinks about what happens with a story that ends on an uncertain note.

––––––––

Now, I did say that "John received a package" is not a story, and I think we should define why. Is it because it's not a series of actions/events? Well, it is only one action, and it's not a very interesting one, but let's see if that's true with a thought experiment. Think of a second action or event which could happen to this. Then, compare it to the ones I've put down below, and see what we get. I think if nothing else it will be interesting and enjoyable.

————

So, what are some I could come up with? These were mine:

(1) "John received a package, and inside were two tickets to his favorite amusement park." Now we have the potential of a happy day, and know a little about John. We have character backstory, an action, and an event, giving us an experience.

(2) "John received a package, and inside was a severed head." Now we have a horrific scenario, but we again have action + event = experience.

(3) "John received a package, and then threw it out the window." Now we have some mystery, and two actions, but again, action + action = experience.

(4) If we want to see two events, we'd have to rephrase the first sentence, but for example's sake, I'll do it, inverting example #1: "A package was given to John, and inside were two tickets to his favorite amusement park." A little clunky, but it tells the same story as #1, so event + event = experience.

There are a nigh-infinite number of examples, and that's one of the things I love about storytelling exercises: they give you a starting point, and you're allowed to finish that path however you want. There's something I find so exciting about that.

There's no antagonist in any of these stories, but an event doesn't have to be caused by an antagonist. An event just has to be something that happened to the main character. In #4, John isn't even the doer of the verb, but he's the point-of-view character by default.

So, what is "John received a package," if it isn't a story? Well, it's a piece of information. Okay, John received a package, great. Why should I care? What's the significance of you telling me this? Why is it here, in your story?

Everything in your story is there because you actively decided to place it there. Nothing exists on its own like in the real world. As a storyteller, it is your job to decide what you want to put into your work, but there is a reason you're telling this story, and putting every element into it. If I have an anecdote to tell a co-worker, I'm telling them that anecdote for a reason. However, if I instead tell my co-worker that one of our fellow workers, Pete, died, that's not a story. Sure, there may be a reason to care, but there's nothing else about that. He died. End of discussion. It's a piece of information I've given to the co-worker.

Now, if I said "Pete died, and it turns out he had a fortune in his bank account," I've told a story. One thing happened, then another, here's why Pete's death is significant – and this is key – *beyond just the fact that it's Pete's death.* There is a larger significance to this. If we only said "Pete left a fortune behind," it leaves a question about what happened to him, but there's a story there, along with a greater significance, as we have two actions. Action #1: Pete left a fortune behind. Action #2: Pete departed. Maybe he died, maybe he fled.

All this, from the examples of John's package to those of Pete's death, is to say that there needs to be something more to this than just "this thing happened." "Karen ran, then she walked" fits our definition of story, yet it feels like there's something missing. There's no reason to care about this. Great, she's into fitness, then she took a break on her run. Who cares?

Maybe we need to tweak our definition of story a little bit. I know, I know, I said "we're going to work with it," but we are; we're working with it by tweaking it, as well. If actions and events alone don't make a story, then what does? Well, let's think of all the examples before the Karen one, and think about why those fit our definition. Why do the John ones? What about the one-sentence story from the beginning of this chapter? What makes those significant, but Karen's not?

Well, remember when I said the ideal was a balance between actions and events? There's another reason for that; it's not solely because it mirrors the real world. It's also about call and response, action and reaction, cause and effect, like what I mentioned in the introduction. The protagonist does something, and then the antagonist responds. The antagonist does something, and then the protagonist responds. Why is *this* significant, though? Clearly John didn't have an antagonist, yet his examples from the list would count as stories. *Why?*

Because of *change*. A **character arc** is "the sum of experiences which a character undergoes throughout the course of the narrative which causes that character to change." (Unless it's a flat arc, in which case the character stays the same, though typically the world around them will change.) It's all about change. Therefore, our tweak is this: the action or event has to change the dynamics of the scene in some way. Karen running and then walking has no effect on the scene. Sure, she changes what she's doing, but what does that change do beyond itself in that moment? Nothing. On the other hand, the amusement park tickets give John an opportunity to do something, the head horrifies us the readers (and, we assume, John), and John throwing the package out of the window makes us wonder why he did that. All change the status of the scene.

With the beginning example, the knock at the door changes the dynamics of the scene by contradicting the idea that Elpy is the last person on Earth. It creates what's called dramatic tension. Thus, dramatic tension is the fuel for good drama and for the buildup to a good joke, among others. It's ultimately the fuel for stories in general.

Dramatic tension is also a precursor to a component of all good stories: conflict. Conflict, importantly, is the driver of change, and it comes about through the interaction of a protagonist and a force of opposition, something that opposes the protagonist's completion of an action. There is no conflict in the John stories, yes, but there is the *potential* for it. Hence, that's why I say conflict is a component of all *good* stories. Conflict is not solely a component of good stories, as you can find countless examples of bad stories with conflict, but conflict is required for a good story. Keep in mind, a good story is one that captivates us readers/viewers/players. I don't think any of the stories with John capture our interest, but I would bet that the one-sentence story did. What's that ingredient? *Conflict.* Elpy and Ayeay present the promise of a confrontation. Conflict doesn't have to mean a physical fight, it just means, again, that there is a force of opposition. We don't see the confrontation, but it is implied, like Ayeay's presence and the knock as an event. Your mind fills it in. Now we're getting beyond what makes something definitionally a story and going into the realm of what makes a story good at the barest level.

So, if we're going to proceed forward from here, let's first rephrase our definition: a **story** is "a sequence of intentionally-collected actions and/or events which each change the dynamics of their scene and which also cohere together to convey an experience through a medium to a receiver."

Good? Excellent. Now, let's get into the nitty-gritty of those drivers of conflict: the characters.

Optional Exercise: Flash Fiction

It may seem odd to use these small, one-sentence examples when most of our stories in the world are much longer than what I've presented here. Aside from allowing us to see the barest essentials of story, small, quick fiction is actually something in and of itself. Called "flash fiction," this type of writing focuses on stories of very short length, typically fewer than 1,000 words. The intent is brevity, to create something interesting given a huge restriction on length. Try writing a story within fewer than 1,000 words. When you're done, count the number of actions and events in the story, separating the two into distinct categories and counting them up separately. See how your story checks out in terms of how the two totals compare to one another, and then examine what you've created for its effectiveness as a narrative.

Chapter 2: Characters

So, now we know the basic structure of a story, and have a definition for what it is, but a story is nothing without characters, as well. We cannot have a story without some subject to take action or experience an event. Characters don't have to be human, though: in Jack London's *The Call of the Wild* the protagonist is a dog, and in the film *The Grey* (2012), the antagonists are wolves, opposing the protagonist, played by Liam Neeson, and the group of men of which he's a part.

Characters, however, are more than just the drivers of change. The protagonist (or protagonists; more than one is possible) is our window into the world. Their allies are points of comparison and contrast as well as vehicles for exploring who each other are as people.

Remember what I said in the introduction about history being the greatest story ever told? Well, there's no history without humans. Once we go beyond recorded history, we enter prehistory, but that, and pre-human Earth are no longer the domain of history. Rather, they belong with anthropology, archeology, biology, astrophysics, etc. Just as history is dependent upon the written record, it is also dependent upon humans. The formation of the Sun doesn't require humans for an explanation, but the formation of the Roman Empire does. History has the longest character list of any story ever told.

There are elements of storytelling which are medium-dependent or genre-dependent, but the idea of "the character(s)" is present in all stories. It is universal, perhaps not even because all storytellers are human (that we know of), but because actions necessitate doers and events experiencers. However, not everyone would agree that we can treat all characters universally.

In *Backwards & Forwards: A Technical Manual for Reading Plays*, author David Ball suggests that, unlike their counterparts in the novel, characters in plays are not, in the same way, real. Now, we're not talking about Prince Hamlet existing in the real world or not, because of course characters in plays are fictional, but then, they're no different in that regard from characters in novels. What Ball means to say, as best I can understand, is that play characters are dependent upon an actor to give them life, whereas novel characters exist due to the language within the book.

Despite the book's title, Ball is focused more on plays as instructions-for-performance than plays as literature. His advice should therefore be read in that context, and in fairness to him, actors need that latitude. Play characters (and film characters, to an extent, though films aren't redone with changed casts every few years) are given less fullness by the playwright, the thinking goes, so that actors can squeeze themselves into the role while at the same time being given some freedom to make choices on their own about their character. From the production standpoint, Ball seems perfectly reasonable.

However, as I argued in my college class where we read Ball's book, this is not in keeping with either the theatrical or the literary tradition of plays. Shakespeare's characters have retained their general popularity for more than 400 years. *Oedipus the King* (also known as *Oedipus Rex* or *Oedipus Tyrannos*) is an ancient Athenian play whose composition predates the birth of Christ by a few hundred years, and it is still performed. These plays are literally nothing without their characters, so to say that King Lear is less real than Captain Ahab strikes me as very misguided, if I'm being frank with you.

So, characters are a universal feature of stories. Without them, in fact, the work ceases to be a story at all.

Characters, though, are also a reflection of us, as both storytellers and receivers. They allow us an empathetic view into another world, and therefore teach us about both ourselves and each other. They are our surrogates, and they are our guides. We are them. They are us.

It's important to note, though, that while characters are our view into the story, the way in which we receive their perspectives is also important. While this distinction is more important in written works, where you have a marked difference between first-person (i.e. "I went to the store") and third-person narrative (i.e. "He went to the store"), the idea of perspective shows itself in all stories.

To use an example from pop-culture, let's use *Breaking Bad*, a television show focusing on Walter White, a high-school chemistry teacher who turns into a meth kingpin. (No spoilers, though.) His biggest threat isn't any of the antagonists he goes up against in each season; rather, it's his brother-in-law, DEA agent Hank Schrader. (In fact, Hank could be called the series' main antagonist.)

Remember, however, that to say one is an antagonist is to only say that they are opposed to the protagonist, who is the point-of-view character. Is Walter White a hero? That's for you to decide. But is he the show's protagonist? Yes.

Now imagine that this show instead focused on Hank and his colleagues as they dealt with DEA problems, as they are sometimes shown doing in the actual show. Walter – known in the underworld as Heisenberg – then becomes the series' antagonist, and perhaps one of the greatest revelations in TV history comes with the realization that the antagonist has been the main character's brother-in-law the entire time.

Vince Gilligan, the show's creator, was apparently surprised at how much support Walter White had throughout the show's run, and I think the reason for his surprise is that he mistook the idea of Walter White as a villain as signifying Walter White as the antagonist. **Protagonist-centered morality**, a concept that initially comes to us from video games, says that "audience identification with a protagonist is a more powerful determiner of the audience's allegiance to the protagonist than any actions the protagonist takes." As I've said, stories are about empathy, about understanding the characters.

There are other examples of stories which make several characters the points-of-view for the audience, sometimes even doing so with both protagonists and antagonists of one another, to the point where the question of who is which becomes hard to determine. Ensemble dramas such as *Game of Thrones* and *Westworld*, both on HBO, are good examples of this, the visual-media equivalent of a third-person narrative.

This isn't to say that we can easily map the written-work first-person and third-person narration onto visual or even auditory media as easily, but it just is meant to show that the concepts exist cross-media.

––––––

Now, a secondary consideration I should bring up is regarding how characters based on real people, or even "characters" in a nonfiction story, factor into all this. Remember, fiction is a type of story; nonfiction is another. There are some stories which occupy a gray area in between, but for the most part, those are our two modes. We must consider both to gain a full understanding of the concept of "story."

The "characters based on real people," as well as real people in stories we tell and receive, are still characters, but their relationship with reality is different than fictional characters' relationship with the same. The example of the map in the introduction is meant to demonstrate how history is not the same thing as the past, and the same is true for anecdotal stories we tell one another based on things we've seen or heard about from others. Those stories are not the same thing as the actions/events themselves; rather, as I said before, they are a condensation of those into a narrative framework.

This is not meant to be some postmodern critique of the idea of "truth," mind you. Rather, it is meant as a recognition of the difference between what happened, and how the information about what happened is transmitted across space and time narratively.

For this reason, though, I'm personally not a fan of stories which blur the lines between fiction and nonfiction while not making it clear what is fictional and what isn't. I do not mean historical fiction, wherein events of history are intertwined with fictitious ones, because it's typically clear that, while there may be some historical basis to it, the story is fiction.

A perfect example of what worries me is Truman Capote's *In Cold Blood*. Frequently called a "nonfiction novel," *In Cold Blood* and books like it are similar to historical fiction, but they make less attempt to make it clear what is based on facts and what is based on speculation or just made up. The other issue is that these books often outcompete the books purely based in fact, and therefore cloud the line between the truth and fiction, which should be a concerning prospect no matter the era in which you live.

While this book isn't just for writers, if you are planning on playing with the truth for the sake of telling a good story, I implore you to do so thoughtfully, carefully, and respectfully.

That rant aside, all that is to say that characters are integral to stories in all media. In the following portion of this chapter, we're going to look at character creation, character function, and character arcs.

––––––––

So, let's say you're a writer, and you want to tell a story about people who go hiking in the woods. All right, well, now you have to decide on who these people are. How many of them will there be, what are their names, ages, backgrounds, wants, needs, etc.? Creating characters involves understanding your story, and understanding characters in stories you experience means simultaneously understanding the story in which they appear.

Character creation is a process you engage with in all stories you tell, even if it's just a story you tell to your friends about a co-worker. As an example, I'll present the following:

My father once told me a story about his mother's uncle (related by marriage, not blood), called John, and of her brother, named Joe (related by blood). Now, Joe worked with his uncle John, though I can't recall the specifics of their work. At some point, though, it involved Uncle John cleaning a toilet stall, so he calls in Joe. Joe comes in, and sees that whoever last used the toilet hadn't flushed, and there's a big pile of feces in the bowl. Now, here's where John says:

"You know, Joe, some people, they like the smell," pointing at the turd. That's the punchline.

Now, I'm betting that you probably didn't find that very funny (if you did, though, thank you), and I wouldn't have, either. However, when I heard this from my father, I was bursting out laughing. So, why the difference?

Well, it could be that I have a terrible sense of humor, but when I've told several friends this story, they've laughed just as hard. In reality, it has *a lot* to do with the story's characters. (It also is related to medium, but I'd bet there's a way to put this story into written form and make it almost as funny, if not exactly so.)

So, for important background, my dad's maternal family is all Italian, and that includes his uncle Joe and Joe's uncle John. Joe came to the U.S. when he was young enough to lose the accent, but John had a thick Italian one. In reality, the line should be phoneticized more like:

"You knowa, Joe, some-a people, they lika de smella." This is how my dad delivers it.

In addition to that impression, my dad will also gesture with his hands, pretending to *be* John as he points to the toilet to make his point. My dad is an actor playing a role, combining auditory and visual performance into one whole to communicate a character.

So, this story becomes maximally effective with the performance of a character. Like an actor playing a part, though, the character he or she plays does not exist, but is given life through performance. John and Joe were both real people, but by embodying them both, more exaggeratedly John, my father created a new version of each one. They became characters.

Not everyone tells stories this way, imbuing character into their very words, acting out a performance. That's okay. It doesn't make it any less of a story. What my dad understands is how to make a story more engaging by adding those elements, which grab attention. What he understands is how to create characters.

––––––––

In both fiction and nonfiction stories, one has to also consider the function that each character plays in the story. Extraneous details, including characters, must be removed, if they truly are extraneous to the purposes of the story.

This may seem very rigid and not in line with a good portion of stories, but it is. Every character serves a purpose. In stories with massive casts, some of which only have a line or two, those characters are typically employed to add flavor to an overall location. This is one of the components that go into the notion that "the city itself is a character," or some such similar phrase about a story's location.

There is an expectation that every element of a story has *some* purpose, or else it wouldn't be in the story. If I were telling you about a knight on a noble quest, talking about his stop at a local farm to milk a cow would tell you that I have a purpose to this digression. If it doesn't have one, the last logical resort is that it is in there as a joke, or a subversion. There is no point, that's the point. (However, subversion can *very* easily backfire, so be forewarned.)

Regardless if a character seems extraneous to some, most, or all readers, the storyteller almost always has a reason for including them. A truly extraneous character (or other element) displays a greater misunderstanding, one that fails to grasp the basics of storytelling. The issue is not with the character's inclusion in particular, but with the teller's lack of craft.

Still, all characters must justify their inclusion in the narrative in some way. Tellers must understand why each one is included, and know for certain that they belong. We can break characters down into categories:

- **Protagonist**: the focal character or characters, the one whose point(s)-of-view we'll be following in the story.
  - o **Deuteragonist**: term for a secondary protagonist, but one who is not as central of a focus as the main protagonist(s) (hence: second*ary*, not *second* protagonist).
  - o **Tritagonist**: a rare term used to describe a tertiary protagonist, one who is even less of a focus than the protagonist(s) and the deuteragonist(s).
- **Antagonist**: the force(s) of opposition to the protagonist(s), not necessarily even a sentient character (e.g. weather)
- **Foil**: a character introduced to contrast with the protagonist or antagonist; in some cases, the protagonist and antagonist can be viewed as foils for one another.
- **Supporting character**: somewhat self-explanatory; a character whose role is to provide support to either the protagonist(s) or the antagonist(s), while not themselves being a focus. (Ex. love interest, friend, mentor, etc.)

- **Plot utility character**: a character whose sole purpose is to advance the plot, and has no purpose beyond that (ex. redshirts in *Star Trek* media).

I'm sure there are more, and that's not meant to be an exhaustive list, just a way of breaking down characters into some core functions for their stories, though obviously, some can fall into more than one. Their roles are based on point-of-view, as well as their wants (and, possibly, needs) in the story, i.e. the things they desire.

Wants vs. needs is an important paradigm in dramatic theory, which simply states that good stories are always or at least very often about characters who want one thing but then end up learning, in the course of their character arc, what they actually needed. Like with three-act structure, I tend to not focus on this not because I think it's useless, but because I don't find it particularly helpful from an analytical standpoint of narrative in general. Those and other concepts like them were developed when studying theatrical and cinematic drama, and they reflect those origins. We're going beyond that here. However, we'll be dealing with some of this in the next chapter.

As a reminder, "hero" and "villain" are about morality, not function, and while the functional attributes are universal, classifications of morality can shift between cultures. For instance, to the Ancient Greeks, the mythical figure Odysseus was a hero, though not entirely because he was the most upstanding person ever. By contrast, the Romans saw him (under the Latin name Ulysses) as a despicable trickster, and tied their foundation myth to the Trojans, whom Odysseus was celebrated for helping defeat through the use of the Trojan Horse deception. Heck, in Dante's *Inferno*, Odysseus is shown rotting in one of the deepest circles of Hell for his actions during the Trojan War.

Stories will always be just as much a product of their contemporary culture as they are an expression of a universal human impulse.

———

Finally, we come to character arcs, which are decidedly not universal. To reiterate but simplify, a character arc is simply the transformation which a character undergoes from the beginning of the story to its end. Not all stories have character arcs in the sense that a character learns something about themselves or the world, which is how it is often defined. My dad's uncle and grand-uncle didn't learn anything, except maybe Joe learned that some people like to smell their own turds and that Uncle John was a little wacky. In fact, in our definition of story, character arc is nowhere to be found.

In reality, character arcs are an old feature of fictional narratives, going back in the West to at least Ancient Greek tragedy, though the feature has been adopted in nonfictional areas such as biographies. In Ancient Greece, there was no such thing as public education as we know it, and one of the ways the Greeks taught their morals to their public was through drama. Hence, character arcs. Characters suffer so you don't have to!

Like an evolutionary adaptation which is naturally selected and passed on, this idea of a character arc has made its way down through the millennia to us. It works. It creates empathetic characters and compelling drama—when used correctly. Character arcs, like characters themselves, reflect us, specifically our lived experiences.

Think about some of the most profound experiences in your life, and think about how they changed you as a person. Now think about how different you are from yourself years ago, or even when you were a child, however far back you can remember. As humans, we learn, and we change, sometimes for the better, sometimes for the worse. But we change.

The main difference between us and characters isn't fiction, since I'm including nonfiction in this, but in condensation. We change slowly as humans, both as individuals and as a species (and sometimes, this is very much to our detriment), but characters undergo their changes in a two-hour, season-long,

300-plus-page, time span. It's condensed, like history. Biographies condense a lifetime into a book or, on rare occasions, a few of them. So, character arcs exist in real life, but it takes a skilled hand to cultivate it into a condensed experience.

––––––––

Characters drive the story forward through their interactions with one another, through the paradigm of interacting actions and events which we've previously discussed. Conflict arises from them. Without conflict, without some opposition, without some reason for the characters to make the choices they make, there is no story. Regardless of era and medium, characters are a core component of narrative.

Optional Exercise: Fan Fiction

Although often denigrated for several reasons, fan fiction (the writing of original stories in established fictional universes, almost always using pre-established characters) can be good beginning practice for original storytelling. For this exercise, choose a character or set of characters from a story you enjoy, and then, create a story featuring them interacting with one or more characters of your own creation. The purpose of this exercise is to get familiar with character creation by seeing what you can do with what's already been established while practicing using what you've created on your own. Pre-created characters already have a personality and a role, giving you a model off of which to work.

Chapter 3: Setting

Aside from me in the last chapter, have you ever heard someone say that the setting of a story is itself a character? It's often said when talking about, for instance, Batman's Gotham City or the cities in noir fiction. This is not to say that the setting is literally a character in the same way that Batman or Sam Spade is, but that, rather, the setting of a story acts upon the characters in the same way that other characters do.

While in some stories this stands out, causing people to comment that the setting is a character, this is in fact the case in all stories, just more subtly: setting affects the plot and characters. Think about a horror story, and where these are often set. What are some common elements? Isolation. Darkness. Supernatural beings and events. There are others, and not all of them appear in all horror stories, but at least some of them appear in each one. Could you have a horror story set on a crowded street? Yes, but you'd probably have to have it so that the only person able to see or know of the horror is the protagonist. Isolation is still baked into that idea, as long as it's still a horror story.

Setting is often tied to genre, sometimes intrinsically; by definition, you can't have a post-apocalyptic story set in a world that hasn't experienced an apocalyptic event. While we'll deal with genre in a subsequent chapter, just know that often it and setting are tied together, though this is most certainly *not* a rule. Science fiction stories often take place on other planets, with futuristic technology, but science fiction can just as often take place on Earth, and not even in the future; sometimes, science fiction stories are roughly contemporary or even set in the past.

Before we get into more of the specifics, we'll say our definition of **setting** is "the place or places in which a story takes place, defined by physical location, time period, and the restrictions that are placed upon the plot and characters by the place or places."

Now, that definition isn't to say that those three characteristics are always well-defined. In our example from Chapter 1, the world's shortest horror story, we don't know an exact physical location or time period. We know that there is a door on which something can knock, implying that Elpy is inside some kind of shelter. We're also told that Elpy is the last person on Earth, so by implication this is a time period after some cataclysm, so, assuming you reading this are not the last person on Earth, the story is set sometime in the future. Because this story is only a sentence long, there isn't enough time to really see how the setting affects Elpy, so that has to be left more to the inferences of the reader. However, in the interests of giving an example, I'll say this: when I think about the story, I feel the psychological torment that might come from feeling isolated, and then I feel the horror at the sound of the knock.

All stories have settings. In fact, if you don't believe me, try to write a story without a setting, and then return here (don't read on), and see what you come up with. I'll wait.

————

So, how did it go? Were you able to come up with a story without a setting, based on your understanding of setting? Let's find out. Now, while I can't read your mind, nor could I fit all possible stories in here, I'll show you how my thought process went when trying to do this same exercise myself.

So, my thought process began with the fact that I couldn't describe anything about where the characters are. Okay, great, but then, that means they can't really exist anywhere real, since even if the setting isn't described, it would still have an effect. All right, then the character has to be in a blank setting, with all-white walls. Maybe there's someone else there, or maybe the character is alone. A second character's presence or absence would affect the kind of story being told, though.

Well, now what? In order for it to be a story, there has to be a series of actions and/or events, which means that, if the character is alone, he or she will have to comment on this isolated space, because that is all there is. If there were two characters, they'd have to move within this space to interact. Either way, this lack of a defined setting would definitely play a role in the story.

All this is to say that, if you have characters, which you need for a story to happen, then you will therefore *always* have some kind of setting in which those characters exist. The level of importance placed on the setting is up to the writer, but the setting will always be there, in some form, because setting is intrinsic to what a story is; the two are inseparable.

––––––––

Now that we've dealt with that, there is one more important component of setting that we need to deal with before we move on. Whereas location and time period are self-explanatory, the third element of our definition, "the restrictions that are placed upon the plot and characters by the place or places," is a bit more vague, intentionally so. Setting has the ability to affect the characters, and it almost always does.

A simple example is a story about a family experiencing hardship due to environmental conditions, forcing the parental figure to make difficult decisions regarding whether they will stay or go somewhere else to try to find a better future for themselves and their family.

Did I just describe the plot of John Steinbeck's *The Grapes of Wrath* or Christopher Nolan's *Interstellar*?

The vague outlines of this story may not be unique to one complete story, but the *differences* between those two complete stories speaks to a setting's ability to act on the characters. In *The Grapes of Wrath*, the characters go west, from Oklahoma to California, in search of a better future there. They can pick up and move to a different part of the country. On the other hand, in *Interstellar*, the main character has to board a spaceship and search for a new, potentially habitable planet, because the current one won't last very much longer.

The differences in both the environmental conditions as well as the time period place different restrictions upon the main characters. Both are going through hardship, but in Steinbeck's novel, there exists a kind of promised land on Earth, regardless of how it turns out; in Nolan's film, that promised land isn't completely assured, and it lies far beyond Earth.

Imagine a story wherein the environmental conditions of *Interstellar* mixed with the time period of *Grapes of Wrath*. You're no longer talking science fiction, you're talking apocalyptic, because these characters don't have the technology to seek out a newer world beyond Earth. Hence, the different restrictions affect the plots and the characters of the respective stories.

Lest you think this is restricted to fiction, however, think about your own life. Often, when we imagine living in some previous era of history, we imagine it as if we've been teleported to that point by time travel. This is a completely understandable way of thinking about this concept, but, logically, this isn't how it would work.

In reality, we are all shaped by the settings in which we grow up, our personalities shaped only in part by genetics. Think about this: how would your experience of the world change if, instead of growing up when and where you did, you grew up on a plantation in the American South before the Civil War? What if you were the child of the landowner? What if you were the child of slaves who were forced to work that plantation?

Or, what if you were raised in a family that believed homosexual acts were sinful, which would have been the case in pretty much all families for most of Christian European history? How would that change if you were raised in Ancient Greece or Rome, societies tolerant of homosexual acts (even if they wouldn't have had a concept of sexual orientation)?

This is not to make a judgment about the morality of any of those scenarios, because slavery was and is a disgusting institution, regardless of how one's society feels about it. Same with intolerance of others based on race, gender, sexual orientation, etc. However, these happened, and still do.

We are shaped by the society in which we are raised. Even if one rebels against that society completely, that still holds, because that society is affecting the rebel by providing something against which to rebel.

This is why biographies start with the subject's childhood, how they were raised. There may be different motives for doing this, but the first setting we real-life people experience is the one or ones which we inhabit as children. Just as we are not isolated from our world, neither are our characters from theirs. They, too, shape and are shaped by their circumstances, with varying degrees of agency. It is no wonder they reflect us, both individually and societally, in ways both similar to and different from us.

Optional Exercise: Creating a Setting

We established in this chapter that setting is intrinsically a part of all stories, and in Chapter 2, that all stories have to have at least one character. However, for this exercise, we're going to discard any concern for characters. Instead of writing a story, create a setting – and only a setting – by either drawing or describing it. This setting can be anywhere, with anything in it, *except* for characters. There can be the implication that characters were once here, but they cannot be shown or described themselves. I'll let you decide beyond that. In films, TV shows, and comic books which require a lot of detail, often people will be hired to create concept art, essentially giving a general idea of what the world in the work will look like. Think of this as a kind of concept art for a story you may create in the future.

Chapter 4: Structure

So, when we went over the basics of what makes a story in Chapter 1, we were looking at the structural elements, the basic building blocks of narrative, and we went further into depth on characters as a special element in Chapter 2, and setting as another special element in Chapter 3. However, an important distinction needs to be made between those basic building blocks and the structure itself. The components build the structure. In this chapter, we'll be dealing with the latter.

Another important distinction needs to be made between "story" and "plot." These terms are often used interchangeably in everyday life, and we can distill their commonly used mutual definition as being the events of the story. This is fine in general conversation, because it's likely that everyone knows what you're talking about when you use either one.

However, in narrative theory, these two terms represent related but distinct frameworks. Story and narrative generally mean the same thing, and that's how they're used in this book. We can make the distinction between these two and "plot" as follows: story is the events as they play out to the receiver, while plot is their logical sequence. As always, we'll use an example to better illustrate this idea.

Christopher Nolan's film *Memento* is considered an outstanding work of 21st-century cinema, and its often lauded specifically for its unique construction (I'm trying to avoid saying "story" or "plot" here), with good reason. You don't have to have seen the film to read what follows, and I won't be spoiling anything; however, a short explanation is needed.

Memento follows an amnesiac man with short-term memory loss trying to find out who killed his wife. One sequence is presented in black-and-white, and its events follow chronologically, while the other sequence is presented in color and proceeds from the ending backward, with the finale of the film being the two sequences meeting in the middle.

In applying our distinction to *Memento*, we can say that the plot of *Memento* is the black-and-white sequence, then the color sequences if they were played in order, while the story is how these events are shown to the viewer. Plot is about the logical progression of a narrative, while a story is how those events are conveyed to the receiver. *Memento* itself is a story, but its plot points cohere together to form the plot.

In many stories, the "story" itself flows in the same direction as the plot does, and so, this distinction becomes unnecessary. The two terms overlap. Whenever I use the term "story," before or after this moment, it will be in reference to the way the receiver experiences the events. Plot is not our focus here, though it will come back throughout this book at points.

———

Another element of narrative structure that needs to be dealt with is how a story is delivered to the receiver. This is not the same thing as medium, which will be dealt with in the next chapter and which is the vessel through which a story is experienced. Rather, the *how* in this case refers to what we can call the "rhythm of delivery." In this arena, we have three options for categorization: *serialized, episodic*, and *standalone*. As always, we'll go into depth, and then illustrate with examples.

Serialization is "the process of dividing a story into several chunks and delivering them piecemeal to the audience." Now, depending on who you talk to, serialization can also necessitate a division in time between each chunk's delivery, meaning that books divided into chapters are not serialized. For our purposes, we won't mandate that, but we'll keep it in mind.

An **episodic story** is one "that is told in chunks," like serialized stories, "but each chunk is distinct from the others." Some common elements such as main characters can carry over from story to story, but those are our only bits of continuity. Think of these like individual episodes in a TV sitcom.

Finally, a **standalone story** is one "a story that is a complete work (meaning it has a defined beginning, middle, and end) and stands by itself." This is not to say that there can be no sequels to the work, but the work must be able to stand on its own to fit into this final category. Before commercial pressures in the post-Renaissance age made sequels more and more common, standalone stories were incredibly common, and still are, especially in the realm of stories we tell to friends and family about our own lived experiences.

So, what about those examples? Well, while we see serialization in literature, we see all three of these categories readily in television, so we'll use this medium as our example for all of them. We'll start with serialization, or serialized stories. Our example will be *Breaking Bad*, the same example I used in the previous chapter.

In *Breaking Bad*, a single story is followed from the first episode to the last: the progression of Walter White from meek high-school chemistry teacher to drug kingpin. There are subplots which focus on supporting characters, such as Hank, Walt's brother-in-law and DEA agent (who could also, as I said in Chapter 2, be considered the main antagonist of the show), but Walt is, as I said before, the focus of the story. Yes, Walt. Not Jesse Pinkman, even if audience sympathies tend to switch to Jesse as the show goes on. Walt's decisions set the show's plot in motion, and are the main driver of it throughout.

Now, the reason I brought up that example about serialization requiring those chunks of story to be discretely delivered is because of how audience response changed. *Breaking Bad* aired one episode per week each season, but when it and shows like it came to streaming service Netflix, a new phenomenon was born: binge-watching. People could watch whole seasons in a couple days, and plow through the story. The bigger-picture elements of the story could fuse together more succinctly, and people could view *Breaking Bad* as a whole work.

People were admittedly able to do this before streaming, with DVD collections of TV shows. However, the difference is that streaming services began to create their own shows. Netflix would release its shows a season at a time, to encourage binge-watching. Not only were these shows not meant to be watched one episode per week, they also weren't structured around providing breaks in the action for ads to play, like in traditional TV. These two differences meant that the need for an episode to have a beginning, middle, and end was less important, and shows began to act like extended films. Streaming changed everything.

This also happened in printed works, and not just with comics. Charles Dickens pioneered Victorian-era serialized fiction, whereby he would publish his novels in installments through his own periodical, and then collect them into a full novel for publication once every installment had been released. (Those who owned all the individual issues would also sometimes have someone bind those issues into a book.) Dickens's novels bear hallmarks of their serialized origins, including their short chapter lengths and quick plot developments. He was also able to change aspects in later chapters of novels based on reader feedback.

It was like Dickens was writing a 19th-century TV show. In fact, there exists a story of people waiting at the docks in New York for the next installment to come in from London, shouting at the boat's crew to ask if a favored character was dead, having been left on a cliffhanger in the previous installment. Sound familiar? (The term "cliffhanger" itself actually comes from a serialized novel from the Victorian era, where a protagonist in Thomas Hardy's *A Pair of Blue Eyes* is left hanging off a cliff at the end of a chapter.)

With the second category, "episodic," we will use the example of the long-running police procedural *Law & Order: Special Victims Unit*. Each episode, with some exceptions (which became more common in the seasons after the departure of character Elliot Stabler), focuses on a new case to be handled by the officers of the Special Victims Unit, a Manhattan bureau of the New York City Police Department tasked with handling crimes related to sexual assault and child or mentally-disabled victims. The cases change, and each episode has a definitive beginning, middle, and end, but the cast remains the same from episode to episode; cast departures are also acknowledged and explained. The main cast is the continuity.

At the extreme end of this are **anthology** shows like *The Twilight Zone* and *Black Mirror*. An "anthology" series is a television show where there is a different story *and a different cast of characters* in each division. There may at the most extreme end be a cast and story change halfway through a single episode. However, for the most part, we can divide anthology TV shows into two categories: **seasonal anthology** and **episodic anthology**.

A seasonal anthology show is a show which has a cast and story change every season, such as *American Horror Story*. These shows can actually fall closer to serialized than episodic in their storytelling. On the other hand, an episodic anthology show is one which has those aforementioned changes every episode. These are the extreme cases because their only continuity is the show itself. Rod Serling introduces every episode of the original *Twilight Zone*, but he falls under that category of "the show itself," as do the genre and tone of each episode.

Now, the third category, "standalone story," is rarely found in television, which in the United States developed its industry around creating open-ended stories, to keep viewers coming back every episode so that the businesses could make money from selling ads to companies. The best examples of this in terms of TV are one-off specials as well as made-for-TV movies. Feature-length films from back in the Golden Age of Cinema pretty much never received sequels, so films themselves – which TV in the first two decades of the 21st century successfully sought to emulate in quality, popularity, and influence – can also fill in this role for our exemplary purposes.

This is not to say that these categories are rigid and that stories must only be placed into one of them, as evidenced by *Breaking Bad* and Dickens novels. Rather, as always, it provides us with a way to think about function and expression, to understand how stories are structured by their delivery rhythm. These ideas will also come into play when we spend the entirety of the second half of this book talking about medium.

————

If you attempt to know *anything* about story, you will run into the dreaded "three-act structure"; it's taught at conferences worldwide, codified by our most popular media, and insisted upon as not just necessary, but automatic. As natural. Let's first talk about what it is, and then think about its usefulness.

Three-act structure is a way of breaking a story down into its constituent parts to understand how it progresses. Definitions will vary somewhat, but the general idea is that the first act establishes the world of the characters and story, then the second act begins when the stasis of the first act is interrupted in an irreversible way, and then progresses until the climax, while the third act deals with the fallout from the climax (good and/or bad) as well as the story's ending.

You'll encounter other frameworks, such as the four-act structure for writing traditional hour-long TV episodes and the five-act structure seen in the plays of Shakespeare. In reality, these are just the three-act structure with the second act clarified by one or two divisions within it. Three-act structure is the minimum because of the need for a beginning, middle, and end.

The three-act structure's proponents will claim that it arises naturally, not because we're all designing it subconsciously, but because stories require it by their very nature. This is actually a good argument, but it also betrays a fault of the paradigm: it is post-facto. Essentially, this idea was developed by looking at stories and breaking them down to see if there were any commonalities between them, and there were. Writers didn't develop it; theorists did.

My biggest complaint regarding the three-act structure is that it is either too broad or too narrow to be of any use to writers. It's too broad if defined as being beginning, middle, and end, not because that's invalid, but because then, the three-act structure isn't adding anything that we don't already know from understanding that stories have a beginning, middle, and end. It's too narrow in that it's taught to writers as a way to write stories, with certain points that *have* to be in there. In the latter case, it works with film because films always fall around the same length of time, and therefore, it makes sense that you can divide them into three acts.

I just don't find it helpful to writers, and I dislike how it's used. I'm not sorry that I'm tipping my hand here. Three-act structure is a fine if generic way to understand a story that's already been written, but it can be stifling to writers trying to write a story, and in its misunderstood use can easily lead to formulaic storytelling. If you're a writer, practice by experiencing and making stories. You will start to imbue structure naturally, and not be concerned with sticking to a prescribed formula.

Of course, this book isn't just for writers, so I'll say that a better way to think about an **act** as both experiencer and teller is as "a division of drama which demarcates units of the story based on actions or events which change the stasis of the entire narrative." This isn't the only way, and I'm not saying it's perfect, but it's the way I think about an act's purpose in a story. It also meshes well with our definition of story. If we wanted, we could simplify our definition of story based on this definition of "act," to say that a story is "a sequence of acts that conveys an experience through a medium to a receiver."

It should also be noted, though, that the act as a unit of drama in stories is not the same exact thing as an act as a division of a play script that is written into the text, and that this latter idea predates the concept of the three-act structure by centuries. While a play act falls under the umbrella category of the act-as-unit-of-drama, the former is planned deliberately by the playwright, while the latter arises as a consequence of the story itself, regardless of intentional, conscious placement by the teller.

Three-act structure thinking regarding film is useful because the idea of act-as-drama-unit and the idea of act-as-intentional-division (a holdover from the theater) intersect nicely in that, in both definitions, there are three acts to a traditional-length film.

Still, like I said: if you find it helpful, great, but don't let it limit you, as a teller or experiencer of stories.

Optional Exercise: Understanding Structure

Take your favorite story, in any medium, and break it down based on plot points and acts. Use your own determination as to what constitutes a plot point and an act. Ask yourself why this structure you've identified works in this story for you; essentially, ask yourself why, on a structural level, you like this story. If you don't think the structure has anything to do with your enjoyment of the story, then ask yourself why you like it. Either way, think about what you can learn from the structure you've identified and how it can inform future stories you tell.

Chapter 5: Medium

So, when I went to the University of Virginia, I studied in the Department of Media Studies, and received my bachelor's degree in that subject. Often, when asked by people what that subject is, I respond that it's UVA's version of a Communications degree. This is true, to an extent. However, my department was very much steeped in theory, which in this case does not mean an unproven hypothesis, but a framework for understanding how something works. The thing we applied theory to was media, the plural of "medium," which in this case means the method through which information is disseminated. So, let's get into what that means.

Media are about information dissemination, or how an idea is put into your head. As I've said, the spoken word is a medium, as is the written. Media don't have to transmit just stories; in fact, media can transmit pure expressions of their form, such as meaningless sounds, nonsense scribbles, or a video with nothing but a background that changes color. They're all still performing as media even if they're not even transmitting anything that can be made any sense of by anyone. But we still have to define what a medium is, before we go any further.

Using our definition of story and what we've already said about media, let's try to reverse-engineer a definition for what a medium is. We know that media are the ways through which stories are transmitted to an audience, hence the prefix "*med*," indicating something in between. Each medium in fact carries unique properties to transmit stories. So, let's start our definition of medium as the following: "a method with unique properties for disseminating information which differentiate it from other media." It's a start, but we can do more.

We'll apply it to an example I brought up in the introduction: YouTube. One of the top three most frequented websites on the entire Internet, YouTube is home to an unfathomably diverse digital ecosystem of content, and despite some competing sites, it is uniquely dominant in what it does, by far. So, is it a medium? Based on our definition, I'd be inclined to say yes.

However, upon closer inspection, I wonder: is YouTube really "unique" enough to be considered its own medium? It's a video-hosting website, but it seems like the videos themselves are really the medium. YouTube's just hosting the content, it isn't itself the content. The comments sections, as well as the other information you can read on the website, is written, but again, that isn't YouTube. It's *on* YouTube. YouTube could more accurately be called the "**platform**."

So, wait, if the videos and the comments are really the media, then what do we call them? What makes them media? Well, videos hosted on YouTube have to be audiovisual files; they have to be *formatted* a certain way. So, it's the formatting that makes it a medium? No; in actuality, it's the medium-ness that makes it a format.

A medium is defined by how it disseminates information. If we took YouTube away and replaced it with another hosting site but it had all the same videos, the information would remain, whereas if we took the videos away but kept YouTube, the information would be gone. YouTube does not in and of itself transmit information, it hosts the transmissions.

But wait, can't you say the same thing about books? Yes, you could. The physical books are only hosts to the content inside them. But the thing is, when we say "book" as a medium, we aren't referring to the binding or the covers, we're referring to what's inside, the written or illustrated information (i.e. a "novel" when it's fiction; we'll get into more specifics of this in the second part), whereas when we say "YouTube," we're referring to the analogous cover and binding.

So, let's adjust our definition: a **medium** is "a method with unique properties for disseminating information which differentiate it from other media *and* which is indivisible from the information it is disseminating." What that second clause means is that, while you could tell someone in the spoken word what something says in a book or what happened in a film, what you are doing is transferring the information, exchanging it into another medium, but the original information is dependent on that medium for its initial transmission. Again, YouTube can be separated from what it disseminates, video or the written word cannot.

That seems like a pretty good definition for what a medium is. Now that we have that, we can move on to talking about the difference between a story and a medium, and then, how we can broadly classify media into four distinct groups.

––––––––

So, what's the difference between a story, a medium, and the content of the story? Well, let's start with the first two of those three.

While certain stories are better suited to certain media, story is bigger than a singular medium. Story, or narrative, is a framework under which we can classify a certain type of information, whether fiction or nonfiction. Story is about components and their subsequent structure. Medium, as we've already discussed, is how that framework is turned from thought into something concrete and then transmitted to another person.

Uncle Joe had the experience of his uncle John making an observation about human behavior regarding toilet usage, and Uncle Joe then put that into a narrative framework and disseminated it through the medium of the spoken word to my father, who then turned it back into a thought. My dad then had to go through the same process to get that story to me, but his thought, I'm sure, was not the same as his uncle Joe's thought, nor was Uncle Joe's thought the same as his experience of the initial event. (Remember the mapmaker allegory of history from the introduction.)

Okay, but what about content? Well, that's what the story *is*, the actual thing that the framework is applied to and then which is expressed through the medium to the receiver. It's the information, be it words or images. All three – story, medium, and content – work in tandem to provide the entire experience, and without one of them, the experience wouldn't be possible. No content means there's nothing to apply the framework to. No medium means there's no way to transmit the information. No story/narrative framework means that the information is meaningless. All right? Beautiful.

———————

Now, here's where we're going to get into the nitty-gritty elements of media and how, despite their uniqueness, they can still be very broadly classified into four categories. These categories are divided based on the prime sense that interprets them in the experiencer, *not* in the creator. I will now list the four of them, and explain them briefly. We'll go into more depth on these when we talk about media in the second part of the book. The four categories are: visual, written, aural, and interactive.

In the visual category, we have painting, film, comic books, theater, as well as others (none of these will be exhaustive in this chapter). This is listed first because it is the most basic of all the four categories, as it is the only one which isn't unique to humans. All animals experience the world visually, and their *best* understanding of narrative is in visual terms. In fact, the visual category requires no sounds or words at all.

Some media combine, admittedly; film is also aural and its scripts are written, as is the case for theater, as well. Comics combine visual and written. The reason I place comics into the visual category is because of a general rule I'm maintaining about medium classification: the most intrinsic elements define classification under a certain medium category. You can have a wordless comic, but you can't have comic-less words and have those words still fall under the definition of comics. Therefore, comics belong in this category. The same applies for the others which cross media. If you can understand all the actions without something written or heard, then that work belongs in the visual category. These works are associated with the eyes in our paradigm.

In the aural category, we have oral-tradition poems and prose (called oraliture or, oxymoronically, oral literature), music, radio, podcasts, etc. For 90-99% of human history, we communicated solely through speech, writing having only developed approximately 5,000 years before today. These aural works are associated with the ears, which take in the transmitted sounds.

In the written category, we have poetry, prose, scripts, etc. Although arising much later than the first two, writing spread throughout the world to become the nearly-ubiquitous means of communication for humanity. (By "ubiquitous," I'm saying society-by-society. Obviously, there are still many people in the world who are illiterate, in all societies, and a few societies which do not use the written word.) Anything expressed through abstract symbols falls here, as long as it isn't first and foremost visual. These works are associated with the mouth, in that they engage an internal speaker when read to oneself, although this is admittedly not a perfect metaphor.

Our final category, the interactive, is unique in that it requires participation in the creation of the experience, rather than just in the reception of it. Games fall under this category, as does anything else which requires participation in narrative creation. These interactive works are associated with the hands, with the sense of touch, because of their participatory requirements.

This is how we'll divide media in the next part of the book, and it is also a helpful way of classifying media based on both essential properties as well as how they are received by the audience. The only area of the five senses not dealt with is smell (and I suppose taste, since you aren't tasting when you speak). I wonder if there could be something that could engage the nose while creating a narrative framework. (Smell-o-vision doesn't count, since the prime media category is still visual.)

Optional Exercise: Medium Preference

What is your favorite medium for stories, either as someone who tells the stories or someone who experiences them? Is your preferred medium to tell stories different from your preferred medium to experience stories? What is it that draws you to the medium or media that you picked? Once that's done, create the simplest, quickest experience you can create in that medium. Just have fun.

Chapter 6: Genre

So, if you're familiar with any type of fiction, you're familiar with the concept of genre. Whether you're talking about an action film or a science fiction novel, whether you're watching a tragedy or you're enjoying some rock music, you are engaging with that concept. While the idea of genre is more commonly associated with fiction, nonfiction also possesses its own genres, such as the documentary film or the autobiography. As genre is an inescapable component of stories (it's been mentioned a few times in previous chapters for a reason), in order to understand story, we must also understand genre.

Before we define what genre is, though, we need to recognize how genres come to exist. Originating as a French loanword, *genre* is related etymologically to words such as "gender," "general," and "generic," their roots denoting the idea of a group, for classification. You've often heard the word "generic" used to describe something that is basic or non-original, and that definition arises because things that are generic under this sense of the word are classifiable in a broad category. They don't stand out.

The word "generic," however, is also often used to denote something that is part of a genre. When someone talks about "generic conventions," they're talking about the conventions which form a part of a particular genre. In order to avoid confusion in this book between that word as it relates to genre and the word's much more common usage as denoting something "plain," I'm going to instead use the term "genric" when referring to the adjectival form of "genre."

––––––

Genres, it's important to note, arise not out of conscious design, but out of repetition. The concept itself was created as a way of classifying stories into different categories, as a way to understand what they had in common. If the first story ever told is then taken as inspiration for a second story, and then you can find commonalities between them which make them distinct from, say, a third story, you've found yourself a genre.

Determining when a genre is born, however, is often difficult, and this is because of two reasons: scale and inspiration. But first, an example of why things like this are often difficult to determine with clarity. We'll go to history for this one.

I have a question: who discovered the Americas?

At first, you might be tempted to say Christopher Columbus, because that's what's been taught in the scholastic zeitgeist for several generations. (Oh, hey, there's that "gener-" root again. I promise I didn't plan that, it genuinely just arose, though now that I'm saying that I realize that it could also fit into how genres arise. I'll end this tangent.) If you're particularly anti-Columbus, however, you might in fact say the indigenous populations who were there for millennia before he arrived discovered it. They were the first humans to set foot on the continent.

I could argue, though, that since they were almost certainly unaware they were entering a new continent as they crossed the land bridge between Russia and Alaska (or, in some cases, got here in boats by island-hopping in the Pacific Ocean), they didn't discover the Americas, since discovery requires a conscious awareness of the importance or novelty of what one finds.

Another possible answer is the Vikings, who established small settlements in Greenland and Canada a few hundred years before Columbus, and they likely knew they were going someplace new, since their travel was over water, not land.

My personal answer to this question, which was asked of my AP U.S. History class on the first day, was that Amerigo Vespucci, the namesake of the Americas, discovered it. Vespucci doesn't get anywhere near as much credit as Columbus does in popular discourse, but Columbus thought he'd found a new route to Asia, which is why he called the natives "*indios*," because he thought he was in the Indies. (This is also why the East Indies and West Indies are both named as such, despite the fact that the former is in the Pacific Ocean and the latter is in the Caribbean Sea.) Vespucci realized this was a new continent, "new" in the sense that it was previously unknown to non-Viking Europeans.

Now, you could, I think, healthily argue several candidates there, and at the end of the day, it's more of a thought experiment, a question asked to situate the people discussing it within the mindset of trying to parse what it means to live in the U.S. At least, that was the context in which it was asked to my class. In reality, the question of who "discovered" the Americas is less important than the actions taken by those who arrived there; in any case, it isn't really our focus.

So, what does this example have to do with story genre? Well, I can ask a similar question regarding who invented a certain genre. We'll use the science-fiction genre as an example.

Who invented science fiction? Depending on your definition, you could say 2nd century CE writer Lucian, 16th century philosopher Francis Bacon, *Frankenstein* author Mary Shelley, short-story writer Edgar Allan Poe, Jules Verne, or several others. Perhaps you could even go as late as H.G. Wells, though we'll say Verne is the final point at which sci fi could have been invented.

Lucian's *A True Story* is a satire, but it includes outer-space travel, contact with extraterrestrials, and warfare between planets. Okay, so we have some of the most common elements of science fiction, a millennium and a half before even the next candidate listed. Seems pretty solid, right? Well, *A True Story* didn't inspire imitators upon its composition, and therefore couldn't have created the genre. He could most succinctly, perhaps, be called a predecessor to the genre's formation.

Francis Bacon's *New Atlantis* was published in 1626, and presents a vision for the future of humanity, of an ideal society. Between these utopian visions and a heavy incorporation of the newly-emerging field of science, we could very well say that Bacon was creating a genre. However, Bacon's work was clearly at least partly inspired by an earlier work, Sir Thomas More's *Utopia*, so it isn't completely original, though *Utopia* has the problem that it's even less like modern science fiction than Bacon's work is.

What about Mary Shelley? Well, *Frankenstein* is often cited as the first example of science fiction, and it does incorporate both then-current ideas in science as well as speculation for the future implications of techno-scientific development. Also, while it didn't inspire immediate imitators, because it provided the basis for innumerable adaptations, theatrical and, in the 20th century, filmic, it could definitely be called an originator by virtue of its supra-medium influence. However, we encounter the same issue as we do with Bacon, since *Frankenstein* is indebted to, and was originally seen as part of, the Gothic tradition. It didn't originate if it came from an earlier form, right?

Okay, well what about Edgar Allan Poe? Well, he incorporated new and emerging technologies as well as scientific ideas into both his short story "The Balloon-Hoax," and his only novel, *The Narrative of Arthur Gordon Pym of Nantucket*, which in part is based in speculation about conditions about what the South Pole would actually be like. Importantly, Poe *did* inspire imitators, with Jules Verne writing a sequel to *Pym* and with H.G. Wells, another important figure in the development of science fiction, also praising Poe. However, like More's *Utopia*, Poe's stories don't really themselves possess many conventions of true science fiction as it would eventually develop.

Finally we come to Jules Verne, whose stories do possess those aforesaid conventions. He also inspired generations of imitators, as well as numerous film adaptations, including the 1902 short film *A Trip to the Moon*. Hooray, we found him, right? Well, as stated in the previous paragraph, Verne admits to being highly indebted to Poe, so he didn't originate it if he was taking from Poe, just as Shelley didn't originate if she was taking from the Gothic tradition. So, who invented science fiction?

My reason for going on this journey of investigation is to demonstrate that not only is this question somewhat irrelevant, but that it's incredibly hard to pin down an exact answer. Like with the question of who discovered the Americas, it's complicated, and depending on how pedantic you want to be, it varies. Genre develops along a scale, and is inspired by earlier genres and works as well as from real life. Science fiction arose just as much from real-life developments as it did from earlier genres.

Genres can also begin as **subgenres** (i.e. existing as a subcategory within other genres), and then become genres of their own, through frequent repetition and development of unique attributes which differentiate it from its parent genre enough to warrant separate classification. It should be noted as well that works can exist in more than one genre, and subgenres can be subcategories of a mix of genres.

Genre classification is a way of looking at the content of a work, as opposed to its medium, and putting it into a group to understand it in relation to other works. It's convenient, but it is far from perfect. It also arises through both academic and commercial pressures, the latter of which we need to discuss in the following section.

However, before we do that, let's define "genre," now that we have some experience with it. We know that it arises out of repeated usage of conventions, and also that it is a way of classifying works based on those shared conventions.

(Also, while genre is not solely tied to story, we're going to define it in relation to narrative, because that's what we're dealing with here.) So, let's define **genre** as "<u>a category of narrative which is defined by shared and distinct conventions which arises through repeated usage of those conventions</u>."

———

This is going to deal with literature, but the ideas expressed here apply to several media, as I will demonstrate. There is an idea that written works of fiction can be divided into two camps: literary fiction and genre fiction. Literary fiction typically focuses more on character and less on plot, while genre fiction does the opposite. However, if this was the end of it, then the divide wouldn't be as problematic as it actually turns out to be.

These divisions in practice are used to differentiate between "high art" literature and "low art" entertainment, hence the names: "literary" because its focus is on being literature, while "genre" because its focus is, ostensibly, on plot (i.e. the events, which is one of the conventions we can use to define a genre), with the characters of secondary concern. This divide is both elitist and, pardon my language, completely bullshit. Let me show you why.

First, it assumes that fiction which is entertaining cannot ever aspire to be anything more, that it's base and worthy of being looked down upon. This is how entire media, from film to television to comics to video games, have been not only dismissed of being worthy of serious study, but also as dangerous because they take away from more important forms of art.

This distinction hasn't always existed, or, rather, when it has, what is commonly labeled "high art" now wasn't always considered to be that when it was made. The plays of Shakespeare would have been seen as instructions for performance only; the idea of them being high art would have been laughed at during his times. They were written to be enjoyed by a mass audience, like films and TV are. In fact, theater could be called the first mass medium, predating printing by millennia.

However, Shakespeare's contemporary, Ben Jonson, decided to have his plays bound in an expensive type of book called a folio; seven years after Shakespeare died, two of his theatrical co-workers, John Heminges and Henry Condell, decided to do the same with his works, and this folio is the only source we have for about half of his plays. There would be no *Julius Caesar*, no *Macbeth*, no *Tempest*, without this important work.

(It's important to note, in fact, that the term "playwright" arose as a pejorative term by Jonson. Most playwrights of that era would have considered themselves "poets," as they frequently, though not always, wrote dialogue in poetic verse. The term later lost this negative connotation, but its usage attests to a strain of elitist distinction even back then. Also, playwrights from that era who were educated at universities looked down on Shakespeare, who was not university-educated, seeing him as an interloper. Again, this high art/low art distinction has been around for a while, admittedly, even if not in the same exact ways it exists today.)

This idea of printing plays was a radical notion at the time (because printing was expensive and associated with "important works"), yet Jonson's example started a movement that eventually led to plays being viewed on the level of literature. Think about this. When you read a play, you're reading instructions and treating them, not the performance they instruct, as art. I'm not arguing against doing this, but when you think about it like that, it's easier to see how radical this idea was, and how truly revolutionary it has been.

Well, how did theater (not plays, but the performances themselves) come to be seen as high art? Because newer media took its place, from films to TV to comic books to video games. Theater also became more expensive, making it less accessible to the masses. Both of these pressures legitimized theater, and while we have mass-appeal shows that become well known and we also teach theater in middle and high school, theatrical revenue is dwarfed by its newer counterparts. Theater is no longer both a mass and commercial medium like it used to be.

Film has undergone the same process thanks to the advent of television, video games, and the Internet, which all give a pedestrian contrast that makes film seem more and more like a high-brow medium. However, in film as in literature, there is this notion of "cinema" (i.e. the films that win acclaim and awards) versus "movies" (i.e. the films that appeal to the masses).

Now, this isn't to say that all works of fiction are equal, but it is to say that the way we traditionally think about this is wrong. I propose that, instead of a literary/genre, cinema/movies binary, we instead use a scale. On the one end, we have entertainment, on the other, art. Works can be classified on this scale based on how much they focus on character vs. plot, or however else we differentiate between the two ends of the scale. In fact, I have a saying about **art versus entertainment**: "<u>Art is meant to make people inclined to forget remember, while entertainment is meant to make people inclined to remember forget</u>." In essence, art is meant to make us think, to remind us of what it means to be human, while entertainment is meant to be a diversion, a distraction from the world. There's nothing wrong with the latter idea inherently, but I don't think it can be both at the same time to the same person. You can see *Avengers: Endgame* as either a fun ride with heroes or an examination of how humans try to move on from unimaginable tragedy, but I don't think it can be both at the same time for the same person.

All this is to say that I think there is value and validity to works often dismissed as being purely entertainment or for the masses, and I have a problem with the elitist form that this dismissal often takes. Also, I think it's important to recognize how our view of works can change with hindsight, or with succeeding generations.

————

One final point I want to make about genre is its relationship to medium. Genre is not form, despite the frequent claim to the contrary. Medium is form. Genre is the categorization of the stylistic expression through that form. At the same time, however, genre is often inextricably tied in with its medium of origin.

For example, the action genre developed in film because film is able to visualize quick movements and make that thrilling and immediate in a way written works never can. The stealth genre of video games (wherein the player tries to take down enemies without being detected) can only arise through interactive media, because it requires player participation. In the former case, action films definitely influenced action video games, so genres are not always tied solely to their medium of origin, but their development is dependent on that original medium.

Optional Exercise: Crossing Genres

Using whichever medium you like, create a story that combines two or more genres. How do these fit together? Do they clash in some way? Have you possibly created a new (sub)genre?

Chapter 7: Tone

I guarantee that if you've heard anything about criticism of narrative works, you've heard talk about tonal consistency or lack thereof in a work. "Tone" is a very versatile word, but as it relates to stories, it refers to the idea of a story's atmosphere. More succinctly, we can say that it relates to the emotions that it evokes in the audience. In fact, we'll just outright define it, rather than spending this chapter arriving at that definition. **Tone** is "the story's atmosphere, defined by the emotions which it evokes in its audience."

I can already foresee two problems with our definition, but instead of trying to hash it out and arrive at a new definition, we'll instead show how these problems can be solved while keeping our initial definition intact.

The first problem regards the fact that we've placed the determination of a work's tone in relation to the audience, rather than to the work itself. This is a judgment I've made. In understanding works, you can analyze them in relation to the creator, the audience, the world at large, or solely as it relates to itself. In this case, I've chosen to place the audience at the core of our understanding, because of my belief that a story is only complete when it is received, not when it's created. Even if the audience is just the creator receiving their own work, the audience is required for a work to be complete.

The second problem is related to this first one: what happens when you have two conflicting audience responses to a work? What's the tone if one person finds it comical and another person finds it tragic? Well, perhaps then that means the work in question has trouble with its tone, what I alluded to earlier as "tonal inconsistency." It may also be that the work has a different reception between two different people *because they are two different people*, as some works do, though this is not due to tone itself, and therefore is of little concern to us here.

Tonal inconsistency, though, is not the same thing as having two different tones within the same work but at different points, such as a dramedy, which has both dramatic and comedic moments in it. There are works that can walk this tightrope well. There are many others which stick mostly to a single tone. Both of these can be successful.

Tonal inconsistency is when the work is sending conflicting emotional messages to the audience, either because it tries to balance several tones but doesn't, or because its creators didn't have a clear grasp on the work's tone in the first place.

How and if a work is able to balance multiple tones, or is coherent with its tone overall, is not something completely objective. If it were, perhaps then we as a species could be closer to all thinking the same thing about each and every work that exists. People have different responses to creative works; that can't be forgotten. I'm not writing this so that we can make value judgments about subjective responses to creative works. I'm writing this so that we can understand what stories are and how they work. I'm talking about tone so that we can understand its role in this process, which I believe can be objectively understood.

So, there we go. Tone is about emotional evocation. Let's talk about the specifics.

———

Because of its relationship to emotion, we have to incorporate an understanding of emotions into our talk about tone. Because of this, it becomes the case that, just like genre, it's difficult to do an exhaustive list of possible tones, depending on how specific you want to get. For instance, is there a unique narrative tone related to schadenfreude (the malicious joy taken at the pain of others)? Also, is it possible, unlike genre, to have a narrative tone that exists only because of identification, even if it hasn't been intentionally used as part of any story? I don't know. In this case, I find the question more intriguing than any single answer to it.

While we may not be able to create a complete list, perhaps we could still find something valuable by thinking about some of the most basic emotions and how they factor into a story? As an expediency, and for fun, let's start with the five basic emotions depicted in the 2015 Pixar film *Inside Out*, personified as characters inside the head of an 11-year-old girl. As a refresher, the five emotions are: joy, sadness, anger, fear, and disgust.

Joy, which we could also call happiness, is pretty broad, but I think we could agree that you can find it in comedies. Comedy, by the way, is a genre, but it is also a tone. There is the film genre of comedy, for example, and subgenres such as the romantic comedy or action comedy. However, comedy is also tied not just to narrative conventions, but to emotion. It's about things that are funny, light, that tend to make people happy rather than sad. This is not an ironclad rule, but a general convention.

Sadness is something you'll find in tragedy, which, like comedy, is both genric and tonal. In tragic stories, characters who are mostly good experience a fall from grace due to a fatal flaw. In Shakespeare's *Macbeth*, the title character begins the story a masterful warrior who has just won victory in battle and who is loyal to King Duncan. However, when Macbeth receives a prophecy from three witches that he will be given a new title from the king and this proves true, he and his wife begin to give credence to a second prophecy: that he will become king. The rest of the play follows Macbeth's ambitions, spurred on by his wife, turn him to regicide and then into a mass-murdering tyrant. It is this ambition, which is Macbeth's fatal flaw, that drives the play's tragic forces, and results in his downfall. It's all, most importantly, driven by his own actions.

It should also be noted that comedy and tragedy are not the only genres where you will find those respective emotional tones (when they're approached as genres), but that these two categories have been around since Ancient Greece, and therefore have a long history behind them with which to apply these ideas.

Fear is a bit more specific of an emotion, on display in works of the horror and thriller genres of fiction. Works in this tonal atmosphere make the audience afraid, either for themselves (if it relates to real-life issues) or for the characters inside the story, or both, in certain instances. To return to our example from Chapter 1, "the last person on Earth heard a knock at the door," the story elicits fear because it introduces an element of the unknown, and contradicts previously-believed information. Who or what is knocking on the door? Is it a ghost? Is it a monster? Is it in fact another person, contradicting the idea that this person is the last on Earth? We don't know. That makes us fearful.

Anger is an emotion invoked more often in nonfiction stories, especially those associated with a political or social cause. The mobilization of anger is done because it gets action done, regardless of the morality behind those actions. This often includes stories of national conflict against another, outsider force of people. It is this narrative, it must be admitted, which has justified countless atrocities throughout human history, such as the Holocaust, which was perpetrated through a national narrative of Jewish people being a threat to "true" Germans. The tone of totalitarian rhetoric is always anger (although it gains effectiveness through fear), and while I love narrative, at the same time I have to acknowledge that just as it can be a powerful tool for social good, it can also be used for its opposite. The key question is who uses that tool, and how they use it.

Anger, as I've said, can also be used to make people work toward a common good, or help draw attention toward a previously-ignored problem in society. Causes focusing on racial or environmental injustices are particularly notable for this, mobilizing anger about these injustices to get people into the streets to protest and, the organizers hope, into the voting booths to enact change in leadership, assuming that the current regime doesn't respond to their concerns.

Finally, we come to disgust, which is, like fear, a bit specific, though I'd argue even more so. You can find it in works intended to make one, well, disgusted. Look at gross-out humor, or horror films which focus on gory details, the latter of which have garnered the distinctive subgenre title "gorno" (i.e. a film emphasizing gore in the same way a pornographic film emphasizes sex).

There are, as I've said, many more tones to be dealt with, if we wanted to get into more specifics, though I think these five act as good illustrative examples of the concept.

Optional Exercise: Tone Swap

Create a story where the tone changes every time a sentence changes or you go to the next panel (if you do a comic). You could instead swap the tone after a certain amount of time, perhaps even swapping mid-sentence. A third option is to do this with a group, where each one of you switch after a certain number of sentences, panels, or amount of time.

Chapter 8: Theme

Ah, "theme." The scourge of English students everywhere. How many times is this question asked by English teachers to students: "What is the theme of this work?" and how many times does it elicit groans or at least silent frustration? It's like you're being asked to play a guessing game, trying to read the mind of both your teacher and the author, who may very well be long dead and not have been particularly interested in talking about their specific intent regarding the themes they inserted into their works.

To be completely honest, this frustrated me as well when I was a middle-school and high-school English student. To me, stories were written to be enjoyed; "literature" was a punishment that took certain works of fiction and placed them on a higher pedestal so that students could be tested on their understanding of that work in ways that aren't explicitly revealed in the text itself. I still find myself asking: at what point does a work become "Literature" in the capital-L sense? (Even though I said I thought the divide between this and genre fiction was bogus, I do still wonder what criteria others use to make that determination. The answer, in my experience, varies.) Unlike mathematics and science, there is no exact metric for determining this, just like there is no exact metric for determining a work's theme (or themes; works can and very often do have more than one).

A theme can be placed in a work intentionally by the author, or perhaps it can be found only with the hindsight of history, the author and contemporary audience completely unaware of this theme. For instance, although it wouldn't be identified as a mental disorder until the twentieth century, certain critics read post-traumatic stress disorder into Homer's epic poem the *Odyssey*, as it becomes hard for its main character, Trojan War veteran Odysseus, to leave the war behind him. Homer (who probably didn't exist, and if he did, didn't compose the works attributed to him by himself, as they were originally composed orally by many poets) and his audience probably weren't aware of what PTSD was, even if some of them experienced it, but with the advent of modern psychology, modern readers can notice that theme.

This is to say that theme shouldn't be dogmatically imposed upon students so much as it should be something they notice through careful study and independent thought. Sure, perhaps students need to be introduced to the concept by teachers, but I only discovered my love of thematics by reading, watching, or playing works on my own. I wonder how many others have abandoned critical thinking about stories because they find this rigidity off-putting. I completely sympathize with that point, and am in fact eternally grateful for my teachers who managed to walk the line between saying what a theme was and teaching me how to find it myself.

So, if themes are so diverse that they can be the product of authorial intent or they can arise independently of that intent, through the understanding of the audience, then what is a theme in the first place? Let's define **theme** as the following: "an idea which is explored through the story and which becomes core to the understanding of the work by the receiver."

Before we go into specifics, I want to make it clear that theme is distinct from **motif**, although they're often used together, sometimes interchangeably.

A motif is "<u>a recurring symbol or concept which is shown to the audience and</u> <u>which helps develop one or more of the work's themes.</u>"

So, for example, a theme would be "guilt," but a motif would be the recurrence of carpets, which remind the main character that they wrapped up their murdered spouse in one and used that carpet to dispose of the body. A theme is intangible (and not explicitly stated, hence why some people can find different themes in the same work), while a motif is something a receiver can point to in specific.

On that note, we need to define one more thing, **symbol**, as it is integral to our definition of motif. A symbol is "<u>a concrete noun, such as a person, a</u> <u>place, a color, an object, etc., used to represent an abstract noun, such as death,</u> <u>chaos, aging, etc.</u>" When a symbol repeats in a story, it becomes a motif.

It's arguable whether or not all stories have themes. While symbols and motifs are placed there normally with intent, and are feasible due to the increased complexity found in planned, artistic or commercial stories, a theme is a very broad concept. Even in advertising, you can find a theme. So, do themes come up in all stories? To be honest, I don't know.

My initial answer was going to be "no," that like symbol and motif, a theme needs some room to develop, and therefore, stories like that of the last person on Earth or of my dad's Uncle Joe and Grand Uncle John don't have themes. In fact, I had this whole argument for you about it. But as I was arguing why "the last person on Earth" didn't have a theme, I was doing what I've done throughout this book: looking for counter-examples to prove my assumption wrong. I asked myself if someone could find a theme in the world's shortest horror story, and I thought, well, how about the theme of isolation? "The last person on Earth" is an image that conjures up the most isolated character of all time, which we mentioned in Chapter 3. Do you feel his or her isolation in the same way you do with, say, Tom Hanks' character in the film *Cast Away*? No, but it is there.

How about my father's story? Well, sure, maybe the story isn't saying anything very profound, but what about this theme: the comedy of human behavior? What I mean, more specifically, is the idea that human behavior can be inherently funny, that human beings are odd creatures, characters who are themselves fascinating because of their weirdness (and we're all weird in our own ways).

So, there you go. It seems like all stories have themes, even ones the author wasn't aware of. Perhaps this is because themes inherently arise due to the combination of the actions/events cohering together and our understanding of the real world (which includes our inborn skill at pattern recognition). We fill in those gaps, and therefore we find the themes even if we're not aware that we're finding them, even if they weren't placed there with intent. Maybe this is another reason why we humans love stories so much.

A story's theme is what makes it more than just a simple record of what happened. Even history has themes, some arising because of how we choose to organize history, others arising out of recurring, real-life human behavior.

However, I will be the first to admit that stories that are constructed with themes consciously in mind have been the most impactful to me: the video game *The Last of Us* and the graphic novel *Watchmen*. These works were created with specific intent, crafted with care and intelligence on the parts of their creators. Their themes, for me, capture the complexity of what it means to be human, and this is done in two media which have been – and still somewhat are, as of this writing – looked down upon by the mainstream. These works changed my life and my view of the power of stories. They mean something to me, and, judging from both works' popularity, to many other people, as well.

In my view, the point of English teachers is not to tell you what to value inherently as much as it is to show you why we as a culture value the works that we do, while hopefully helping you to develop your own power of reasoning so that you can make these determinations for yourself, in your own life. Not paternalistic, but guiding. My favorite English teachers are those who have been able to do the latter, and who inculcated within me a passion to which this very book's existence is indebted.

This is the power of thematics.

Optional Exercise: What's the Theme?

What's a theme or the theme in your favorite story? If you and one or more friends have also experienced this story, do they have different ideas about what themes stand out to them (assuming, to be fair, that you can get friends to talk about this in the first place)?

Chapter 9: Why Stories Matter

In compiling this first half of *Narrative in Action* on the components of stories, I've taught myself some things about narrative that perhaps I knew subconsciously but had never put into words before, or things I didn't know at all. Putting together this section has also made me think about what stories mean to me, and why I think they're important.

In Chapter 7, I spoke about how you can understand a work of fiction, and in some ways any narrative, "in relation to the creator, the audience, the world at large, or solely as it relates to itself." In terms of works being understood solely in relation to themselves, this is the same idea as "art for art's sake," that is, art produced for aesthetic purposes. Harold Bloom, a literary critic known for advancing the idea of the Western canon of great works of art, believed that works should be approached solely as works, and that trying to understand them in relation to politics or sociology was ruining art.

Now, I respect Bloom, if for nothing else than I believe his concern was genuine, his motives were pure, and he didn't strike me as a hypocrite. (His work regarding how artists deal with the influence of their predecessors, expressed with in his book *The Anxiety of Influence*, is something I highly and uncomplicatedly admire.) However, I disagree with the idea that *only* Bloom's listed works are worthy of study. As I said in the chapter on genre, it took Ben Jonson publishing his plays to bring respectability to the medium, and to prompt the production of a book which preserved Shakespeare's plays. Opinions change. And yes, perhaps works that are popular now won't prove to always be that way, and there is something to be said about works being judged by how they survive time.

However, Bloom's "Western canon" does not include any African or Asian authors, and he does not have an equivalent work which talks about those cultures' works on the same level. What Bloom seems to argue is that these works and *only* these works are worthy of being studied on a worshipful level. I don't agree. I think stories can be very impactful, and very personally or culturally important, even if they're not universally adored or studied. I think there's value in certain works of most or all media, not solely literature.

The reason I bring up Bloom is because of my disagreement with him on art only being understood in relation to itself. I respect this frame of analysis, but I definitely disagree with it being the only one used. Now, returning to the second paragraph, if we drop the aesthetic frame, we still have three: the author, the audience, and the greater world.

We can rephrase these three modes into a paradigm: **intent, reception, and effect (IRE)**. The intent of the work is the creator's perspective, what they intended the work to mean, and what they wanted to say with it. Reception is the audience's perspective, how they interpret the work, even if they know what the author's intent was (though often they don't). Finally, the work's effect is its influence beyond the audience, into the world at large. Sometimes these three overlap neatly, but very often, all three diverge.†

---

† Sometimes, an audience member's reception can turn into their own intent if they make something inspired in some way by what they've experienced. This is how ideas are spread and passed down in the first place.

As we always do, we'll use an example. This time: animated-Disney-movie villains. For this example, we'll stick to films animated traditionally (i.e. by hand) released by Walt Disney Studios in the eighties and nineties. But first, one more definition: **coding**. In film terms, coding is when characters are given characteristics which connote ideas about those characters in the audience's mind without saying it explicitly. **Queer coding** is when this process is used to connote that the character in question is LGBT+ (lesbian, gay, bisexual, transgender, etc.) without saying it.

In *The Little Mermaid* (1989), the main villain is Ursula, a masculinized octopus character whose look was based off of a drag queen from the era named Divine. She is shown, in her scenes with the main character Ariel, to have an almost sexual attraction to her. If Ariel does not woo Prince Eric in three days, Ariel will be a possession of Ursula's. The film ends with the heterosexually masculine Prince Eric ramming into and destroying a gigantic Ursula with a ship. Thus, the queer-coded character is killed and balance is restored.

In *The Lion King* (1994), the main villain is Scar, the younger brother of the current lion king, Mufasa. Scar is given feminine mannerisms, including a lisp, feminine hand movements, and a flair for the dramatic, as well as other characteristics which connote him as gay. (However, I am not saying all gay people have these characteristics, or that having these characteristics makes someone gay. What I'm saying is that the association was and is still common, and therefore, the connection was there to be made in the minds of viewers.) With him in power, the land becomes barren, a reflection of an unnatural leader. Is he unnatural just because he killed his brother and ordered his nephew killed, or also because he is gay? Is his villainy caused by his "deviance"? Order is restored once Scar is violently killed by his own henchmen and Simba, confidently heterosexual thanks to his wife, Nala, becomes the rightful king.

Connoting queerness as a way of making it clear that evil characters are unnatural and therefore different from the always-heterosexual protagonist is a tradition tied back to the early days of cinema, when censorship codes wouldn't have allowed for sympathetic depictions of gay people. Even in the eighties, queer people were demonized as unnatural, made worse by the AIDS crisis and its association with gay men. Only in the 21st century have these issues begun to be rectified in notable ways. Still, these ideas influenced these depictions of Disney villains.

Another example of connoting is done racially. In *Aladdin* (1992), the story takes place in a fictional country which is some mix of Indian and Middle Eastern (already problematic) which is called barbaric in the opening scene (more problematic) where the main character, Aladdin, is given features of a white man, especially in his facial features, while in contrast, the villainous Jafar's eyes are heavily slanted, the most in the film. Aladdin is white, Jafar is Middle Eastern. Like it or not, the film is making a racialized statement.

In *The Lion King*, the queer-coded Scar is depicted as holding a Nazi-like rally with the hyenas, all depicted as subservient to him. The three hyenas who get lines – voiced respectively by Whoopi Goldberg, Cheech Marin, and Jim Cummings – are connoted, through the chosen actors as well as voicework, as African-American, Hispanic, and mentally handicapped, respectively. So, the minorities and the handicapped side with the queer villain, and with them in power and part of society (i.e. integrated, treated like everyone else), the world is turned upside down. The world becomes unnatural. Meanwhile, Mufasa (who is voiced by an African-American, but James Earl Jones's voice doesn't code as African-American here like Goldberg's does) and his straight, white family are rightfully meant to rule over the Pride Lands.

There are other examples, such as Pocahontas's Native American heritage connoting that she is more in touch with nature, or Esmerelda in *The Hunchback of Notre Dame* (1996) being exoticized because she is a gypsy. However, I think I've made my point.

Now, was it the intent of the filmmakers to say anything like this? Well, I don't know, but my guess would be that it wasn't. They just imbibed what they saw in films or experienced in real life when they were growing up and put that same language into their own movies. However, the effect is to draw an association in people's minds between queer or foreign characteristics and villainy or some other stereotypical characteristic, upholding longstanding and very problematic ideas.

In the case of queer-coded villains generally and those in Disney movies particularly, though, the reception part is where things get interesting. While mainstream audiences probably didn't consciously notice the queer coding, queer audiences often did. However, because of the dearth of queer characters on screen generally, members of the LGBT+ community turned these villains into gay icons, their only examples of people on screen who were like them, even if they were villains. So, the intent was neutral, the effect was negative, but the reception for the affected group was sometimes positive. Understanding works of fiction and their origin as well as effect is complicated. I'm not saying that these films should be thrown onto the fire and burned, but I am suggesting that we should all be more conscious about what stories are, what they say, and what their impact on us as receivers is.

Stories matter. They inform us about what happened outside of our immediate experience, and they help us express to the younger generation what our society's values are. They unite us together; seeing *Avengers: Endgame* in the theater with my best friend and his girlfriend was an experience I'll never forget, and the moments of triumph hit harder than most other films have for me. Stories are also used to divide us, by promoting ideologies which seek to oppress a group of people to the benefit of another, to justify the existence of bigotry and hatred.

Finally, stories help us make sense of the world. Who we are, what our purposes are. Just as they unite us, they keep us going in hard times and remind us of who we are. They let us express or experience our hopes, our loves, our frustrations in another avenue, helping us to understand them better than we could just by direct experience. Stories are about empathy. They make us feel human. They make us human. This is why every society to ever exist, going back beyond recorded history, has told stories orally, or painted on cave walls. They say: "This is who we are. This is what matters to us. This is our stamp on the world. We are here. We matter."

It's thoughts like these that remind me of why I love stories, these little bits of magic that are transmitted to others and evoke sensations, whole experiences, within them. It's why I'm writing this book. So, thank you for coming along with me on this first part of our journey. I hope you'll continue to stay with us. However, I want you to always remember this: you matter. Your stories matter. You are part of the human experience. I hope, in whatever form, you can share your stories, too.

Optional Exercise: Why Do You Care?

Ask yourself: what is about your favorite story or stories that makes you love them, that makes them stick with you? What stories have influenced the way you see or think about the world, and how and why did they have that effect on you? Why do stories matter to *you*?

Part 2: Medium Analysis

Introduction to Medium

So, while we spent a whole chapter defining what a medium was and its general implications, this second half of the book will focus on the topic in particular, looking at media from the four large narrative-media categories (visual, aural, written, and interactive). Whereas Part 1 was about aspects shared by all stories, this part is about the differences in stories as determined by medium.

So, as a refresher, our definition of medium is "a method with unique properties for disseminating information which differentiate it from other media *and* which is indivisible from the information it is disseminating." We arrived at this definition in part by differentiating a medium from the physical platform that holds that medium and allows it to transmit its message. YouTube is the platform, video is the medium, the content in those videos is the message. (When I use "message" in this sense, by the way, I mean it in the sense of "transmitted information" generally, not in the normal sense of a specific bit of information. So, it can be plural.)

In Chapter 5 of Part 1, I said that a book was a platform, but a novel was a medium. As promised, I'll get into that here, because it helps illustrate the admittedly somewhat nebulous difference between the two. Think of a novel that you either like or know about well enough to make some general statements about what's inside the binding.

So, what makes that thing a novel? Well, we might be inclined to say the length, and that's a fair criterion. The question is, are we basing it on page count or word count? With page count, the actual length depends on the size and type of font, as well as the size of the pages themselves. This is one of the main reasons why English teachers mandate a certain font type and spacing length for papers that have a page-count requirement.

With word count, on the other hand, you have something that's fairly standard, though there are differences depending on how one counts, for example, hyphenated words like "self-reflection." Certain literary awards typically define a novel based on word count, saying that a novel must be at least forty-, fifty-, or sixty-thousand words. However, this metric only works if you know the word count. For books, most readers don't know the word count, but they know the page count; they can just look at the book's last page to know.

So, if our definition of a novel is that it's a long book of narrative fiction, that's great, but it doesn't help us define what it is in specific. It's the "I know it when I see it" standard. So, is there anything else that makes a novel distinctly a novel?

Well... what about chapters? A **chapter** is "<u>a division in a book that separates content into sections, thereby differentiating the content in that section from what comes before and/or after it</u>." Chapters aren't solely used in fiction (heck, even I use them in this book), but when it comes to novels, almost all of them have chapters. (Some exceptions exist, such as the chapterless John Bunyan book *The Pilgrim's Progress*, which is sometimes called the first English-language novel. Bunyan is also of no relation to Paul Bunyan, a lumberjack figure in American folklore.)

So, yes, I'm tying the definition of "chapter" to a platform rather than a medium, but that's because, as I just said, chapters don't just appear in novels.

However, as I said, almost all novels contain chapter divisions, which in that case serve to split up the story. Chapters aren't defined by page count or word count so much as they are by function. A chapter is a unit of story, with its own beginning, middle, and end, following up on something from a previous chapter (if it isn't the first chapter) as well as setting up something to happen in a subsequent chapter (if it isn't the last chapter). Other media express divisions of story in different ways, it's just that chapters are the ones most often and most visibly used with novels.

Remember as well that a medium is defined as both a method for disseminating information and as something that is indivisible from the content it transmits. Well, the method has to have unique properties, or else it falls under a larger heading. So, does a novel in the non-physical sense fit our definition of medium?

Well, a novel definitely has unique properties in its usage of chapter structure, but its length could also be counted as a unique property. (However, without defining a minimum length, there is no exact way of determining this.) So, the first criterion is satisfied, but with this alone, all we know is that the novel is at least a platform. We have validated the novel as a physical object, but is it a medium? To answer that question, we must ask: is the novel indivisible from its content? Yes. I'll demonstrate why.

Have you ever read a novel, then watched a film adaptation of that and said that the novel was better? If you have, then you've just demonstrated that a novel does satisfy the second criterion. Film has unique properties which distinguish it from the novel (it's visual), from comics (it has aural components), and from television. The last is the most important, because film and TV are often compared.

So, what's the difference between film and TV as media? It's not where they're watched, because streaming services have both. It's their rhythm of delivery, a concept introduced in Chapter 4 of Part 1. TV is serialized, with distinct chunks of story called episodes. Film is a monolith, one story, across (typically) 90 to 120 minutes. This isn't to say a film can't have subplots, but that once a film is over, all of its plots are resolved. It may have sequels, but those are separate units, whereas episodes of a TV show all come together to constitute one work.

Even the megafranchise (i.e. a franchise of franchises) known as the Marvel Cinematic Universe, often compared to a TV show, follows this pattern. Yes, it has sequels, yes its films are intertwined, but each franchise, and each movie within each franchise, is a separate work, with their own beginning, middle, and end. Granted, the MCU does blur the line a bit, more than most other film franchises, but while *Iron Man 3* is dependent on *The Avengers* for an understanding of its story, it features a definitive end for Tony Stark. You could watch *Iron Man*, *Iron Man 2*, *The Avengers*, and *Iron Man 3*, and you'd have a complete series. There is nothing within those works necessitating you to come back beyond them. This isn't how TV works, at least with non-anthology shows.

So, film delivers a single story. Well, so does a novel. But a novel has episodes called chapters. A film doesn't. So, when adapting a novel to a film, screenwriters have to not only cut, but restructure the story to fit a new medium. Stories are influenced by the medium in which they are created, and thereby will always best suit their original medium. The reason film adaptations ever work is because the story is changed enough to fit the filmic medium while still satisfying viewers. A novel is more like a TV show, a short story more like a film. I guess that means that a short film is analogous to flash fiction. (Or we have to recognize that analogies aren't always perfect.)

A story made for the novel will, aside from rare exceptions, be structured around chapters, with ebbs and flows in the story such that each chapter ends something as well as begins something else, unless it's the first or last chapter. A novel's story is dependent upon the novel's structure to exist. Therefore, the content is indivisible from the novel, therefore the novel as a non-physical entity is a medium.

By the way, this idea of a medium being as or more important than the information that it transmits isn't an original idea of mine. In fact, this idea has actually been around since the 1960s, when media scholar Marshall McLuhan published his book *Understanding Media* (1964), in which he coined a now-famous phrase, "the medium is the message." McLuhan felt that it was more important to study media (i.e. the plural of "medium") than it was to study the messages within those media. McLuhan is in many respects a founding father of modern media studies, and this book you're reading now almost certainly wouldn't exist without his influence.

––––––––

In the pages to come in this part of the book, as we delve into the specifics of each medium category and medium therein, we are going to encounter nebulous terrain, where questions like "Is a novel a medium?" but for different formats will come up. We like to categorize the world into neat little patterns, but the world often finds a way to defy our attempts at categorization. There's always an exception, there's always some gray area, and by shoving things into a specific category, sometimes we force a classification that doesn't exactly fit. We aren't perfect.

However, as we go through our exercise, I want you to remember why you love stories, and to think about the medium's influence on your favorite story. As always, I hope you will gain a greater understanding of the forces of narrative.

I have just three more things to note before we begin. The first is how I've decided on organizing this section of the book. We will start with a medium category, then go by time of medium invention (or an approximation), all the way until we get to the next medium category. I've decided to start with the visual category first, because it's the oldest one of which we have a record.

The second thing to note is that I will use examples to demonstrate each medium when I feel it's needed. The examples in question will be what I am familiar with. You may not be aware of these examples. That is completely fine. If you wish to think of your own instead, feel free to do so, and follow along with the work that I perform using my example. I wish this could be interactive, and I could use your preferred example each time, but alas, this isn't a work written in an interactive medium, nor would it be possible to write something interactive using the perhaps billions of total possible examples when factoring in all media we cover.

The third and final note is to reiterate what I said in my chapter on medium: while I acknowledge that many media cross the traditional categories I've established, I have to put them into some category. My general rule is that the most intrinsic elements define classification under a certain medium category. Interactive media form a separate category, but any medium with interactivity is automatically placed in that fourth category. This is also why it's the last category.

So, let's get into it.

Last Optional Exercise: Medium Practice

This book is for people who create stories and those who enjoy experiencing them, though I assume if one enjoys creating stories then one also enjoys experiencing them. However, these optional exercises have been created for those who wish to create, as an extra bit of content to help creators hopefully hone their craft. This is the last exercise because we are going to get into specific media in this section, and my exercises would be the same for each: try to make something in this medium. So, I make this one final exercise: try to make something in each medium, if you have the ability to do so. Even if you don't like the medium, gaining an understanding of the unique processes of each medium can help you gain a better understanding of stories as a framework, and, hopefully, help your own processes, regardless. However, as I said in the exercise at the end of the chapter on medium: *just have fun.*

Section I: Visual Media

Introduction

We humans are a visually-oriented people. It's been that way throughout the history of our species, and it's a trait we inherited from our evolutionary ancestors. It's because of this, as I stated previously, that I've begun with visual media. Before humans had language, long before we had the written word, we had visual information. We could see the movements of the prey we hunted, and communicate visually with our group members through what we could see. Even when hunting a prey in silence, we could coordinate visually. (We may have also developed the visually-based sign language before spoken language.)

As we progressed into the spoken language, ideas became divorced from a need to demonstrate them visually, and abstract concepts could be developed. Interestingly, despite the fact that we denigrate lying in our society (though I'm not saying we shouldn't), the ability to lie is associated with more advanced brains. Beyond that, in fact, the ability to tell fictional stories, which in a sense are complete lies, comes from our development of language.

In the 21st century, we are assuaged constantly by visual information, so much so that only a few generations back it would've seemed like our modern world is one of science fiction. I cannot stress this enough: our visual culture is

84

not some aberration from the norm; it's in fact a modern reinvention of a preliterate society. Visual information is so immediately salient to us humans because it's something that's been salient to us for the entire half-million years our species has existed, as well as before that, for our evolutionary ancestors.

From paintings to comics to film to online video, the history of narrative visual media in human societies is long and complex. Visual media are also our longest-lasting intentional record of human existence. So, without further ado, let's start with an art that's tens of thousands of years old.

I.1: Painting, Drawing, Sculpture

So, let's say that you're part of a hunter-gatherer society around 40,000 years ago. Whether you're hunting for meat or foraging for plant-based foods, this doesn't occupy you for the whole day. Sure, it's strenuous, but your group needs this to survive, so you do it, chipping in, helping out, whatever you need to do.

Then, the end of the day comes, and your roaming group needs to find shelter, if even just for the night. Your group comes across an opening in the rocks, and a few of your hunters, possibly including you, go into the cave to see if there is any threat lingering within. Once the cave has been cleared, the rest of the group goes inside. Your group is small enough for the cave to fit everyone.

Then, the next day, you wake up, and see that it's raining outside, as well as thundering and lightning. You know from experience that the flashes of light can strike humans and kill them where they stand, so your group doesn't go out in the storm. Some of them gather around a makeshift fire. One of them begins to tell a story, but it's the same one he's told three times already. There's only so much you can hear of how he escaped the big, hairy monster chasing him.

You go off by yourself into a corner of the cave, illuminated by the firelight. You see a small rock on the ground. You pick up, and examine it.

Nothing of interest. So, you knock on the cave wall with it, just messing around, trying to occupy your time. But you notice something: the rock has left marks in the cave wall. You start to use the rock intentionally, making an outline of the cute animal you saw the day before, working from memory. It's crude, but it looks interesting enough, and you feel a sense of pride at it.

Then, a friend of yours comes over to look at it, and finds herself fascinated with what you've made. Pretty soon, everyone else is over, and an idea starts to form…

Eventually, your group learns how to make pigments using iron oxide and other common materials, and they begin using those to create these images, ones which look like the animals with which you're familiar. Someone else has the idea to use hands directly on the cave walls. By holding them up and blowing pigments onto the wall, you've left an impression shaped just like your hand behind.

Tens of thousands of years later, preserved from the elements, your group's artwork is discovered by some intrepid cave explorers (the technical term is "spelunkers"), all of whom are descended from you and other members of the group, though none of them know it. They each grew up hundreds of miles apart, and only met in college. Your legacy lives on.

————

Okay, admittedly that story is pretty much entirely fiction, informed by my understanding of how cave painting worked. The idea of using the rock is, as far as I'm aware, not something the early humans used as an art-making method.

Cave paintings may not seem that extraordinary on their own, and they definitely aren't the most artistically beautiful works ever, but not only do they stand as a testament to the painters' existence, they also represent the beginnings of art. In fact, those two things aren't really that different. While art may in the time period in which it's created stand as an expression of an artist's self, or have some other big meaning, the only big meaning that still survives of those cave paintings is this statement: "I was here. This was what I thought about."

That's the beauty of art. But is it narrative? Not inherently.

Here's where we get into some sticky territory. We've defined narrative as "a sequence of intentionally-collected actions and/or events which each change the dynamics of their scene and which also cohere together to convey an experience through a medium to a receiver." Cave art, as well as both drawings and paintings in general, do convey an experience through a medium to the receiver. That part's true. But in order to be a narrative, there has to be a sequence of events (i.e. more than one), and they have to be significant (i.e. change the dynamics of a scene).

The question becomes, what constitutes a unit of action or an event? It's easy in stories that are explicitly told as such, but what about in painting? On the surface, very often there isn't a story, just a statement, either that this person existed (as in portrait painting) or that, hey, I wanted to make something beautiful. Even in history painting – a genre given that name not because it depicts historical scenes (though it often does), but because it tells stories – it isn't clear if our understanding of narrative fits with it.

Let's take, for example, the *Mona Lisa*, which is a portrait painting, but its ubiquity will help us understand why it's hard to ascribe narrative to paintings. All we know from this picture is that there is a woman, enigmatically smiling, with a landscape behind her. That's it. From a narrative standpoint, that's all we get. In fact, we don't even get the title, since that's not part of the visual category, but of the spoken or written category. So, no narrative.

Even in history painting, what makes it deserving of that title is that it depicts a single moment of a narrative. However, one moment is not a sequence; therefore, by our definition, it doesn't hold up to scrutiny.

Let's take as an example an imagined painting, where a girl in a medieval village watches longingly outside of her window at a man working in the fields. Clearly, she has a crush on him, right? Okay, yeah, and he's doing an action, as well. It's a moment, but there's more than one action, so what gives?

Well, what gives is our need for the dynamics of the scene to be changed by that action. These two actions, looking and working, are unrelated to one another. Well, okay, the looking may be related to the working, but the other way around has no relationship.

Perhaps, then, if he looked up at her, then that would be something? Sure, but if she had the same look, and he were looking back at her, noticing her, it's still one thing. Why? Because the scene hasn't changed. Without the initial setup of him working, the moment of him seeing her has no impact. There's no change. Therefore, no story.

Now, what about information that you bring with you to the canvas? For instance, say that you have a painting of George Washington, and just George Washington. He's dressed in some formal gear, we'll say his Revolutionary War uniform. Perhaps you read into it his adherence to the cause, and his importance to the foundation of the United States. Perhaps, if he were instead wearing clothes more associated with plantation life, you would think instead about the fact that he was a slaveholder.

These are both aspects of George Washington, but neither these nor other readings would come from just the painting. Rather, they would be from outside knowledge we bring into the painting. It is valid to say that these are narratives we bring to it, but it's also important to recognize that *we are bringing this in ourselves*, as opposed to receiving this from the painting.

So, all paintings are just moments then, right? This chapter is pretty much a complete waste of time? Not exactly. See, there *is* actually a way to find narrative in painting and drawing that fits our definition, but it's not a type of painting so much as it's a process. In painting, there exists a concept called **continuous narration**, which is when several actions or events are told in one image. It's called this because while most paintings, drawings, or even sculptures depict a moment frozen in time, works with continuous narration depict several moments in one image.

This technique arises in art because of the very problem we've identified, that static art is limited to depicting one thing, frozen in time. Artists wishing to communicate narrative in their paintings while not requiring viewers to be informed by previous outside knowledge would have to figure out how to fit several moments into one frame. (Unless, that is, they thought outside of the frame, but that's the next chapter.)

Returning to our example painting, which I'll call *Watching the Farmer*, our theoretical painter could depict the scene in such a way that we see both her gaze at the farmer as well as his reaction to her, upon being seen. In a sense, these moments cannot be simultaneous, because one is in response to another, but on canvas, they can be. You'll find this in a lot of paintings, from many centuries back, with the reactions of figures acting as a kind of guide through a painting, so that the movement of your eye creates a narrative from just the information on the canvas. One artist who was particularly known for this technique was Leonardo da Vinci, and in his paintings with multiple figures, this is on particular display.

There is, however, another option regarding continuous narration, this one more traditionally associated with that term than what I outlined above. With this type, the painter could have the farmer in the far left of the frame, working the field, then have him standing closer to the center, looking up at the girl, whose expression remains the same. As long as we could tell it was the same person, and we were aware of the possibility of continuous narration, we'd have a sequence of actions and events, and therefore, a story. You've fit two moments distinct in both time and space within the same frame, but this also has classical precedents, especially in religious works.

In either case, we have a narrative. Yay! Problem solved, right? Well, sure, but what if we wanted to depict several moments? Well, we couldn't, not using this technique. The canvas would be bloated with figures, and it would all devolve into nonsense. The clever cheat of continuous narration doesn't work here.

We've therefore reached the limit of traditional painting, drawing, and even sculpture in regards to narrative. Even if they extended their frames or space, it would still seem like a crowded composition. So, how do artists solve this problem? Well, by applying sequence not only to what's inside the painting, but to the painting itself.

I.2: Sequential Art

Introduction

If you're like I was when I first heard this term, you probably don't know what it means, though its basic definition is pretty self-explanatory: art in sequence, right? Yeah, but the history of this term (not, however, the thing to which it refers) is related not to painting, but to comics. So, before we define it, let's talk about where the term comes from.

So, because of their association with children and superheroes, comic books were, and still often are, seen as a low form of entertainment, with nothing artistic to offer. Eventually, however, more mature work came out of comics and into the mainstream (although there have always been some adult comics), and so comics creator Will Eisner, known for creating the character of The Spirit, coined the term "sequential art" to describe the medium. From what I understand, Eisner used it the way we're going to use it, which is that it referred to a sequence of images used to tell a story.

However, comics creators interpreted this and another term, "graphic novel" (which we'll deal with later in this chapter, actually), as attempts to legitimize the comics form by getting rid of the term "comics." I understand where these concerns are coming from, and I think those who marketed comics did and do employ legitimizing terms like these for that purpose, but I think the terms have actual usefulness, too.

To Eisner, comics weren't the only type of sequential art, they were just the most well-known. This is how we'll deal with it, as well. For our purposes, **sequential art** is "a sequence of images used to tell a narrative." As opposed to continuous narration, these images, it should be emphasized, have to be separated in some way.

Section 1: Pre-Comics

So, this entire chapter is highly indebted to *Understanding Comics*, a 1993 book by comics theorist Scott McCloud which is entirely in the form of comics. For McCloud, comics and sequential art are synonymous. In fact, he uses "sequential art" as part of his definition of what comics is (when referring to the medium, "comics" is singular), but he makes a case that the history of comics goes back millennia, to Ancient Egypt. I disagree on this point; I think *sequential art* is millennia-old, but I think comics are less than 300 years old, at least in the West. We're going to spend an entire section of this chapter on comics. For now, though, we're going to talk about sequential art before comics came around.

So, McCloud argues that the earliest instance is in Ancient Egypt, where murals sometimes recorded distinct events in order, though in McCloud's example they're read from right to left, left to right, then right to left (alternating each row) and bottom to top. He makes a compelling case, but to me, I see continuous narration in this example, because there is no clear separation of images. Same with his example of the Bayeux Tapestry, often cited as an early example of sequential art. Nope, continuous narration once again.

Now, let's return to our *Watching the Farmer* example picture from the last chapter. Now that we've freed ourselves from thinking solely about having to have it all in one picture, let's think about what we could do with the new toolset of sequential art.

Well, in one painting, we could have her watching him work, then in the next he looks up as she waves back. We now have a story, told in two panels. We could continue it on; maybe we have him go up to the woman, or maybe we have him leave the field in the other direction, as she looks disappointed.

In fact, let's play with that first example for a second, of him going to talk to her. Well, what if we not only wanted to show not only *that* they were talking, but *what* they were saying? Well, in point of fact, painters had a way of doing this for centuries in non-sequential art. It's a predecessor to the modern speech balloon, and it's called a "banderole." Banderoles are basically speech balloons, as they emanate from the mouth of the character, but instead of white bubbles, they're parchment-colored scrolls (hence another term for them, "speech scroll"). They serve the same function, though, and, in fact, serve to give a sense of time passing.

McCloud says that the simplest way to give a sense of time passing is to have the characters say something, because we understand that speaking takes time. Therefore, the scene lasts for as long as it takes us to read the speech. On this, I completely agree with McCloud, and point to the banderole as evidence that this understanding existed long before modern comics.

Now, there are many examples where a sequence of images have been employed in the history of art, and we can't be exhaustive about this. However, we must remember that the difference between continuous narration and sequential art is that, in the latter, there is a separation of images, two distinct, independent pictures, not one depicting, say, either side of a wall. There may be a division in the picture which appears to extend outside the bounds of the world of the picture, but unless it actually does, it's continuous narration.

Oh, also, sequential art could also theoretically be used in sculpture, where two works placed side by side depict sequential moments, and therefore, form a narrative. I didn't initially plan on including sculpture at all in this book, but I realized that it should be dealt with alongside painting, since both are similar in that they depict subjects, and are often grouped together classically. Sculpture has also existed since prehistory, like painting and drawing.

Now, we come to our seminal figure, the one who bridges the pre-comic and comic in the history of sequential art in the West: William Hogarth. Hogarth lived in 18th century England, and he is most known for his multiple series of paintings which tell stories. They are – in order of composition – *The Harlot's Progress* ("harlot" meaning prostitute), *The Rake's Progress* ("rake" meaning an immoral pleasure-seeker), and *Marriage-a-la-Mode*. Hogarth was a satirist, and his works highly critique his contemporary society, but their importance to us now comes from their sequentiality. Hogarth originally created the third painting in the *Harlot* series as a standalone work, then was intrigued enough to decide to create paintings depicting where the prostitute came from and what happened to her.

The success of *Harlot* inspired him to create his two subsequent series. Are these paintings comics? No, but was Hogarth the world's first comics artist? Yes; we'll get into why in a second. As they stand on themselves (or, well, stood, since the *Harlot* paintings no longer exist), they are examples of sequential art in painting, perhaps some of the best.

Now, let's get into why Hogarth invented Western comics.

Section 2: Comics

Well, okay, "invented" implies that he did this intentionally, but he didn't, nor were his actions without influence from predecessor people and technology. What happened was that Hogarth created his original paintings in a time when printing was revolutionizing communication once again. Hogarth's original paintings were reproduced using an engraving process, and the copies produced using this process were so popular that they were frequently pirated, leading

Hogarth to push for the practice to be outlawed by Parliament (which it was), thereby also having an impact on the development of copyright.

While his paintings weren't comics, the engraved copies are, based on my definition. So, what is my definition? Well, while some people define comics in relation to the combination of words and images, and others define comics in relation to the sequentiality of images, I define comics in the latter way, but with a caveat: mass production. Or, perhaps, mass *re*production. **Comics** as a medium is "mass-reproducible sequential art." That's my distinction.

Now, this doesn't mean that it has to be reproduced on a large scale to qualify as comics under this definition. Rather, what it means is that sequential art is a comic once it's put into a form that *can* be reproduced on a massive scale. So, for example, if I paint three pictures in the *Watching the Farmer* series, that's just sequential art, but if I draw them so that they can be placed into a comic book, comic strip, printed on their own, or found online (i.e. mass-reproduced), then they become comics.

However, in my view, taking a picture of each one and placing those online would not make the paintings themselves comics. At the same time, comics that are made by hand and then scanned, for instance, are still comics. The important difference is in the intent of the work. Paintings are made to be singular, to stand on their own, even if they are part of a sequence. If they are created in a process that makes it possible to copy and disseminate them widely (i.e. makes them mass-reproducible), then they become comics. A series of images of sequential paintings *would* qualify as comics, but that *doesn't* change the nature of the original paintings.

On the other hand, a page of drawings which is then scanned can qualify as comics for the same reason, that their fundamental nature isn't altered. Assuming that the page qualifies as sequential art (it would have to in order to be a comic), then, because the scans do not alter anything about the drawings themselves, then the drawings are mass-reproducible sequential art, and therefore, comics.

To illustrate why this does not create a paradox, consider instead separate, individual images, each scanned separately. If they were then assembled together digitally, the assembled final product would be a comic, but the parts themselves wouldn't be, because they weren't sequential art initially.

This is somewhat like what the photographer is doing. By photographing all of the paintings and putting those pictures together, they have created a comic, but the paintings themselves are not comics because they, in their original format, are not mass-reproducible. Whether the final product of the sequenced photographs would be a photocomic or a traditional comic is irrelevant; it's the distinction between sequential art and comics that matters.

Also, it should be made clear that while comics falls under the category of sequential art (though I think it's earned qualification to be treated as its own medium), comics are not the same thing as cartoons. Per McCloud, cartooning is a style often employed in comics, but comics can also be made out of photos, like I said. In fact, I made a photocomic using nothing more than my phone and laptop cameras, some photo editing software, and Microsoft PowerPoint. (Yes, I made a comic using PowerPoint. It was actually a very interesting experience, and I recommend trying it if you can and you're curious.) So, *cartooning* is a style, and *comics* is a medium, one which falls under a larger category of sequential art.

One final note is that there is a distinction to be made between illustrated books and comics. To be classified as sequential art, a work must place a primality on images over the written word. A book with illustrations in it is not comics by having illustrations in it; rather, those illustrations must make up a narrative in and of themselves. This is not to say that comics with dialogue or with overhead panels are somehow not comics, but that the *primacy* must be placed upon the images. Children's picture books use images in sequence, but the images play a secondary, illustrative role to the words, whereas in comics, words play a secondary, explanatory role to the illustrations. If images are of secondary concern, then what is telling the story first and foremost is the words, and therefore, the work cannot be sequential art, and therefore in turn cannot be comics.

With the ability to mass produce images, and thereby with the birth of comics, came an explosion of content in the medium, following alongside the success of pulp novels and magazines. Newspapers also began to include story-based comic strips, not just political cartoons or one-off illustrations. In fact, my grandmother's second husband, John Prentice, drew the detective comic strip *Rip Kirby*, originally created by *Flash Gordon* creator Alex Raymond, from 1956 until his death in 1999. So, to be honest, I have a special interest in the history of comics.

Section 2.1: Comic Books, Graphic Novels

So, comics originated in newspapers, and were for a long time just found there. In fact, the name "comics" comes from the fact that most early comic strips were based around jokes, and were therefore "comic." Whereas in other languages the term for comics is related to the nature of the medium, this genre-related term stuck with it in English.

Although the comic book could be said to originate with the American publication of Rodolphe Töpffer's *The Adventures of Mr. Obadiah Oldbuck* in the 1840s, this didn't kick off a revolution like comic books in the 20th century would.

Comic books began as publishers had the idea to make a few bucks by reprinting old comic strips in book form around the early 1930s. Then, in the late 1930s, as content for reprinting was running low, the same publishers had the idea to create original content for comic books, in much the same way (though not for the same reason) that streaming services starting with Netflix began to make their own original content. As National Publications was putting together a comic anthology book (in this case a collection of completely unrelated stories), someone came across a proposed newspaper comic strip that had been frequently rejected.

The strip was by two young Jewish men from Ohio, and it featured a man with incredible strength who performed heroic deeds. The disparate individual strips were then reworked, and one of the images actually made the cover. With the release of *Action Comics* #1 came not only the debut of Superman, not only the debut of the superhero genre, but the beginning of the modern American comic book. (This, combined with the scarcity of surviving copies of the book, is what makes the book, in good condition, worth millions of dollars.)

Now, there's a whole history I'm glossing past here, but if you're interested, go read up on it. It's a truly fascinating story, but one incidental to our purposes. As I said before, comic books gained a reputation as being for children or geeky adolescents, with the superhero genre providing to readers a power fantasy, or wish fulfillment. They were disposable trash, in this view.

Then – although not without preceding developments – comic books changed. In the mid-1980s, three comic books in particular released that altered the landscape forever: Alan Moore and Dave Gibbons' *Watchmen*, Frank Miller's *The Dark Knight Returns*, and the first half of Art Spiegelman's Holocaust comic *Maus*. None of these were works you'd given to children, yet two of them were about superheroes.

In recognizing this change, there was a push to emphasize the prestige of these books, likely as a way for publishers to gain a more adult readership and thereby make more money. Bookstores started hosting a separate section, labeled "Graphic Novels." No longer could you find these just at comic shops.

However, there was pushback from creators, with the concern that the term would be used so that comics publishers could just sell what they'd always been selling but with more prestige attached. (This was the complaint of *Watchmen* writer Alan Moore.) I think this was and is a valid, understandable concern.

At the same time, I also think that there is a need for a term by which to refer to novel-length comics, because "comic book" is in a sense already taken. When I say "comic book," I guarantee that you think of what's called a "floppy." It's bound not with a spine, but with staples. Also, almost always a comic book is one episode in a series, whereas novel-length comics have a beginning, middle, and end.

I'll use *Watchmen* as an example. Originally, *Watchmen* was published as a limited series of floppy comic books; it was a series of twelve issues, to be exact. Once that was done, however, the issues were collected and then, instead of continuing to sell them individually, publisher DC Comics sold them as a book, called a "trade paperback" in the industry.

What do we call this new form of *Watchmen*, as a single work? Well, if we were asking this about a serialized novel like that of Dickens or contemporaries, we'd say that it's just a novel. A Dickens work is now always published as a single novel, as opposed to in its original installments. This changes how we see the work. Instead of waiting for each month's issue, we can read it through at our own pace, and thereby view it as a single work.

In my view, calling the complete *Watchmen* a comic book would be like calling a complete Dickens novel a "chapter." Therefore, I define **graphic novel** as "a spine-bound book of comics content that is in and of itself a complete work." This way, it encompasses both originally-serialized content as well as works created originally as novels. It also divorces the definition from any length requirements. On the other hand, I'd define **comic book** as "a single unit of comics content which is not spine-bound, not a complete work in and of itself, or both." This way, a comic-book can either be its own single issue (in the industry, this is called a "one-shot") or part of a larger work while at the same time still being a comic book.

Finally, since it falls under the genre of comics, I'll define a **comic strip** as "an ongoing comics series published in a periodical not solely devoted to comics." With that definition, though, I want to make something clear. While my step-grandfather's *Rip Kirby* comic strip is being republished in big books (to accommodate the strip's horizontal length), these are neither comic books nor are they graphic novels. Why? Because while they have a spine, they aren't in and of themselves the total work. The *Rip Kirby* series is the total work. Rather, they collect about nine stories apiece, with each story made up of a few months' worth of strips, each day having a three-panel strip (some exceptions of two- and four-panel days notwithstanding).

This collection is a comic album, a term I would also apply to, for instance, *The Walking Dead* collected volumes (even though they aren't shaped like albums), as the total work is *The Walking Dead* series as a whole, not each collection separately. The comics industry has a separate term for this same idea, called a "trade paperback," to which I previously referred. (A trade paperback doesn't have to be the same thing as our definition of a graphic novel.) Either term works for our understanding, as long as we use "graphic novel" for works that are in and of themselves complete, like *Watchmen*.

Before we go, there is one important note that needs to be made about graphic novels and comic books which differentiate them, potentially, from comic strips. Comic strips take as their fundamental unit the panel; in other words, movement from panel to panel is what defines comic strips. While comic books, which originated from comic strip reprints, have this same unit, they, and graphic novels, have another narrative unit: the page.

In the reprints of the three-panel-a-day *Rip Kirby* strips, the panels of day one have no visual connection to the panels of day two (although they obviously have narrative connection), because they were printed on separate days. However, a comic book begins its life as a work wherein the first, second, and further lines are related, because they're designed and printed at the same time. This is how panel design is able to vary so wildly in comic books. It also means that meaning can be baked into the book on a page-wide basis as opposed to just the panel, and seeing the page as an entire unit can allow for a different understanding than just considering the page panel-by-panel.

For example, in comic books, most especially superhero titles, there is the concept of the "splash page," wherein an entire page or two pages (the latter called a "two-page spread") are made up of a single image. This wouldn't be possible in comic strips, and this also shows that comic books don't always require panels to create their narrative. However, this technique is rare because it is only effective when used sparingly, as setting it off from the normal, panel-delineated pages is what makes it stand out and have a big impact.

Section 2.2: Webcomics and Digital Comics

Webcomics fall under the category of comics because they're mass-reproduced, or, perhaps technically, reproducible. They're only reproduced when one accesses the webpage, but regardless, they are able to be reproduced on a massive scale. Either way, they fall under the definition of comics. This is also true regardless of how they're laid out, whether it's more like a comic strip, a comic book, or a single panel per click.

On that note of "single panel per click," the distinction I'm making here between webcomics and digital comics is similar to that which I made between comics and sequential art. All webcomics are digital comics (if they're printed, they cease to be digital in that specific instance), but not all digital comics are webcomics. Both, however, fall under the definition of comics, which means that they in turn fall under the sequential art umbrella. When I created a comic using PowerPoint, with one slide equivalent to one panel, I created a digital comic, but because I didn't post it anywhere online for people to view, it wasn't a webcomic.

Digital comics, for our definition, are comics which have been made using digital processes and which exist in that form, but which haven't been posted on the web to be distributed. If digital comics were posted on the web, they would become webcomics; if they were printed and distributed like traditional comics, they would then become traditional comics. If I merely distribute them privately among friends using email but never post them online, then they are digital comics. They are webcomics if and only if they can be accessed without the person having to receive them from me directly, and can view the comics at their own leisure.

The difference may seem a bit pedantic, and likely isn't the same as it is for others' definitions, but it is the one I think best helps to understand the workings of this subcategory of the comics medium.

Section 3: Conclusion

Now that we've dealt with static images laid out on a page or a screen, we're now going to look at what happens when we make a lot of very similar images and show them in rapid succession to create a sense of movement: animation.

I.3: Animation

So, let's imagine you're sitting out in your garden, shortly before the year 1800. You're a painter, and your portraits are renowned throughout your country, but by now, you've gone into semi-retirement. You've made enough money that you can now take fewer commissions, allowing you to choose your patrons, rather than the other way around.

As you're watching your pet dog run around the yard, you think about the portrait you did of your family, one which included the dog. In that portrait, the dog was lying still, but there was no way you were going to actually get him to sit still for that long. Rather, you just sketched him quickly and separately, then inserted him into the painting from memory. He was just too rowdy to sit for a portrait.

You watch as he chases a butterfly, wagging his tail and jumping up and down. How could you possibly capture *him* in a portrait, with all that motion to deal with? Then, you look at his wagging tail, how in its high speed blur it looks like it's in several places at once. (This phenomenon is called "motion blur," though you wouldn't be aware of the term.) You think about it, and an idea comes to you.

You walk back into your study, grab some paper, and you draw your dog, just once, his tail pointed all the way up. Then, you draw the exact same image, save for the fact that now, the tail is pointed slightly downward. You do this some more, until you've made enough drawings that the tail has gone down and all the way back up. Then, you begin to quickly flip the pages, one after the other, and you notice, to your delight, that it creates the illusion that the dog's tail is moving, in excitement.

You've just become an animator.

———————

Animation is all about illusion. It comes from the root *anima-*, deriving from a Latin word related to the idea of "life." Hence, the related term "animal." Animation is, like its photographic cousin, film (as in the medium, not the physical film used to make a *film*), about motion, specifically creating the illusion of it. Nothing is moving in the real world except for the sheets of paper, or digital images. However, when these things pass by your eye fast enough, it doesn't process these as single images, but as a depiction of a moving object.

This is also what differentiates animation from sequential art. Sequential art is about separation. Whereas continuous narration occurs in a single image, and sequential art allows for the usage of multiple images to depict changes to a scene, animation is about taking a long sequence of images and morphing them into a singular whole which creates the illusion of movement. Though, when the animated images are separated, you could call it sequential art. In fact, regarding a movie recorded on film stock (because the book was written in 1993, before the advent of digital filmmaking), in *Understanding Comics* Scott McCloud says that you could say, before a film is shown, that it is an incredibly slow-moving comic (or, in our terms, sequential art). Same idea here.

So, what's our definition of "animation?" Well, this is actually where it can get a bit confusing. While we've already established that photocomics are a thing, and therefore divorced the idea of the cartoon style from the comics medium, we also have to recognize that, if we analogize that to animation, then all films, even live-action films, are animation.

The problem is, like with comics, we've wrapped up notions about styles of animation with the medium of animation. Just like we can differentiate comics from both cartooning and sequential art (though those terms are related), so too can we differentiate animation from its styles. All we have to recognize is that what makes something animated versus something filmed (i.e. on a camera) is that the images are created by hand, or, in the case of computer-generated animation, through a process of creation and manipulation.

When I say film, in this context I'm talking about what's been called live-action film, a term retroactively applied so as to differentiate films with real-life humans in them from films where the people inside have been created through some artistic process. We will talk about the medium of film (a.k.a. "cinema") shortly, in an upcoming chapter. The reason I began with animation, though, is because we're drawing back to what we've already talked about, to the ideas of sequential art and to painting and drawing.

Using these ideas, combined with the recognition that now animation can also be done (and is most often done now) using computers, we can tie down our definition of animation. **Animation** is "the usage of a sequence of images displayed in quick succession to create the illusion of motion, and the images are created using an artificial process." The "artificial process" distinction is what we're going to use to separate animation from film. Whereas film also fits the first part of the definition, it does not fit the second, as despite the fact that very often filmed images are manipulated through computer-generated imagery nowadays, they're still filmed images. Something in the film really exists and was captured with a camera (i.e. naturally). In order for something to fit in with the medium of animation, that thing has to be entirely created artificially, meaning that nothing in it would have existed without intentional creation.

Three notes: First, this does not mean that animated characters in a live-action film are somehow not animated. Those elements are most certainly animated. Remember, we're not talking about "animated films," we're talking about animation in general.

The second note is that this does not exclude claymation or rotoscoped animation from this category. Claymation is animation done using real-life models, and moving them a little in each frame to create the illusion of motion. The reason these are still artificial, despite the models existing in the real world, is because these models are not acting under their own power, but by the direct actions of others, the same way animated characters made using other techniques are captured.

Rotoscoping is done when an animator traces over live-action reference images or footage, to create realistic movement and/or figures. The reason that rotoscoping is still animation, even if an entire film existed originally in live-action (see Richard Linklater's 2006 film *A Scanner Darkly*) is because the artificial process was applied to it. There would be no movie in that form without that artificial application, and therefore, the finished product is animation, regardless of the source of movement and figures. (Rotoscoping has also been used as reference for actual movements in animated films, throughout the history of animated cinema.)

Third, to call something an "animated film" is to tie it solely to length of the animation. An animated film is a "film" because it's feature-length (i.e. it runs for the length of an average movie). Thus, calling them animated "films" does not refer to medium. If anything, it refers to a sub-medium. It's like the difference between a novel being defined by length versus it being defined by how we defined it in the "Introduction to Medium" chapter.

An animation can last less than a second. So, this definition does not discount the existence of animated movies. In fact, for our purposes, animated movies are shelved with the medium of animation, not the medium of film.

———

For most of the history of animation, the medium involved creating images by hand, then putting them together and displaying them in rapid succession. This process arose in the 19th century, and was likely related to the developments of the Industrial Revolution. In a society of machines, motion is not tied solely to living things, but to processes, as well—processes that, in industry, are driven by human creation.

Humans had always been aware of motion, but the origin of the term "animation" belies this association of movement with life. Even those things that moved in nature but were not themselves alive, such as rivers or ocean currents, were part of a system of living things. The Industrial Revolution disentangled the idea of motion from the idea of life, and therefore likely birthed an obsession with artificial motion.

Think about this: painting and drawing had been around for millennia, but only during widespread industrialization did animation come to fruition. At the same time, photography existed for only about forty years before it too was employed to make "motion pictures." It seems, then, that it isn't the length of existence of the preceding static media that determines how long it takes to develop the motion form of it. (Also, I know this is animation, not film, sorry it comes up so frequently.)

Do I know this correlation is also causation? No, I don't. It's a hunch. Besides, if the causation exists, someone else has already probably proved it anyway. The reason I point these developments out and tie them together is because today, in a world full of video, artificial motion seems like a foregone, commonsense idea, but it wasn't always.

Anyway, the way that animation was done for a long time in the 20th century, when commercial animation became a thing in movies and television, was by using a process called *cel animation*. "Cel," short for "celluloid," allowed for time-saving innovations to animation. Cels are why the backgrounds always look different from the characters in them, and they're why you can tell an object is going to be used or interacted with in some way; the object stands out from the background. Cel animation meant that the background only had to be drawn once and then reused, with only the characters being needed to be redrawn every frame.

There are many other innovations, as well, in the history of animation, such as the use of so-called rubber-hose animation (think Popeye and early Mickey Mouse, whose arms and legs look like hoses and move like rubber), which not only made it easier to draw characters, but thereby influenced the styles of animation themselves. The medium and its limitations will always influence the content.

————

So, that's traditional animation, also called 2D animation. However, with the proliferation of both computing power as well as computers themselves, it became much more viable to animate in 3D using computers. This innovation allowed for 3D-animated movies as well as 3D video games, though since video games require some electronic interface, their relationship with computers was always more obvious. Animation and computers? What?

Short films on computers were possible in the 1980s, but it wasn't until 1995 that the first feature-length 3D computer-animated movie was released, by a studio called Pixar. The film in question was *Toy Story*, which not only put its studio on the mainstream map, but it also changed animation forever. Now, it's rare to find a traditionally-animated film releasing in theaters.

Computer-generated animation works differently in many ways from traditional animation. Whereas in traditional animation you have to draw every frame, in computer animation what happens is that you create what are called "rigs." (These are more commonly known as character models, at least in video games.) These rigs are like puppets. You design them with features that can be manipulated by animators, and so when you're making the movie, you're moving digital models (a.k.a. "assets") around a 3D environment, manipulating a fictional camera around however you want.

Once computer animation became viable, this process meant that it was much cheaper to produce, and it's why the entire industry shifted so quickly to using it.

————

One final distinction needs to be made, and in a way reiterated, before we move on: style. Just as comics are not the same as cartoons, neither is animation. Cartoons are a style of drawing that was adopted in animation and came to be associated with the medium, but they're a style. In fact, "cartoon" is an umbrella term for several distinct but related styles.

Cartoons, however, are a 2D style. Whenever 2D animated characters are rendered in 3D, they look bizarre because you're trying to take something on a flat plane and put it in a 3D one where you need to see something from all angles without it losing its cartoon nature. Cartoons almost never work as 3D models, because they're intrinsically tied into a 2D world.

Don't believe me? There are many examples of this, but if you want really good examples, look up the Nickelodeon *Jimmy/Timmy Power Hour* TV specials, or the *Nicktoons Unite* video games.

When Jimmy Neutron travels to the world of *The Fairly OddParents*, it works much better, because you're reducing what's there, not adding something onto it. On the other hand, when Timmy Turner is in the world of *Jimmy Neutron, Boy Genius*, he looks different from the other characters, and not in a good way. He and the other *Fairly OddParents* characters were designed for 2D, not 3D.

In the first *Nicktoons Unite*, Timmy and Jimmy are joined by SpongeBob SquarePants and Danny Phantom. As Danny Phantom is in the same style as Timmy Turner, he and the characters from his world inherit the same problem of looking lifeless and out of place. SpongeBob fits in better, probably in part due to the many 3D games have been created with him, but in reality almost certainly due to his simplistic design. He's a rectangular sponge. All you need to do to make him 3D is turn him into a rectangular cube. There's no human head or body to have to deal with turning into a 3D object.

Admittedly, these examples are all taken from my knowledge of pop culture, and from my generation. Those examples were released while I was in the target demographic, and you bet I watched or played them. The great thing about the Internet, though, is that you can look things up, so I recommend, if you can, looking up these examples to see what I mean, if you're curious.

Regardless of what you decide to do on that front, though, I think it's time to move on. While film would seem to be a natural jumping-off point from what we've been talking about, if we're going to move from visual media which are wholly artificially created to media which involve some degree of live-action, we're going to need to go further back, because film is indebted to two media for its formation. The first is photography. The other is a millennia-old medium known as theater.

I.4: Theater

Theater is performative. That may be obvious to you, or even, in fact, tied into the very notion of theater so intrinsically that me saying that first sentence seems like I'm treating you like a five-year-old. I'm not. Reiterating base components of media, reminding ourselves to consciously think about what makes a medium distinct, allows us to think about what makes that medium a medium in the first place. So, what makes theater *theater*?

Well, not only is it millennia old, but it, like sequential art, developed in several different civilizations independently throughout history. Modern theater in the Western world traces its origin to Ancient Greece, while other theatrical traditions developed separately in India, Japan, and Africa, as well as in Persia, China, Native America, etc. This multi-society development of theater points to something innate about human nature which lends itself to creating live-action performance pieces.

Before we get into a theory I think best explains the origins of theater, let's think about performance of narrative *before* theater. Specifically, we're going to look ahead, to the aural medium category. Before we had the written language, we told stories orally, in the spoken word. In some cultures, people

112

known as "bards" would memorize and compose poetry to be performed through speech. However, these bards were *telling* stories. They were saying what happened and letting their audience imagine it. With theater, you have people acting out what occurs in the story, *showing* you the story.

The theory to which I give the most credence for the development of theater is that it originated as ritual. Before theater, religious rituals would be performed, sometimes with the actions of the gods being mimicked by the religious leaders. The tradition of oral narratives likely intersected with the religious ritualism of performance to create something new, an idea of acting out, as opposed to merely telling, the stories, of actually embodying the characters.

According to tradition, the Ancient Greek Thespis – from whom we derive the adjective "thespian," meaning "actor" – was the first to ever step out from the ritual chorus and act as a character, rather than as himself performing a ritual. Thus began the start of theater not only in Greece, but in the Western world.

Plays, however, were not seen as simply entertainment in Ancient Greece when they developed. Rather, play attendance was seen as one's civic duty (if one were a male citizen), and plays were used not as diversionary entertainment, but as celebratory of the glory of Ancient Athens. They were also used to expound Athenian morality, to teach and remind the audience of what Athens valued as a society. Plays were didactic. There was competition, and people were asked to rate the work of three playwrights, whoever gained first receiving a prize. So, there was always an element of subjective judgment, of deciding which plays succeeded the most, however that was determined.

Each playwright, who was also the director and often one of the three actors (casts were small), would present a series of three linked tragedies, followed by a comedic fourth play called a satyr play (not to be confused with *satire*, which is a very different genre, and which developed millennia later), as a pallet cleanser of sorts. Later, there would be a separate competition for comedic plays only (though these wouldn't be satyr plays), though unlike with the tragedies, where Athens invited those from rival city-states to come see them, Athens kept the comedic competitions to only Athenians, likely because these often made fun of the state and/or society of Athens itself.

There is only one surviving complete tragic trilogy, called the *Oresteia*, which was written by the playwright Aeschylus. Sophocles' *Oedipus the King* is often paired with two of his other plays, *Oedipus at Colonus* and *Antigone*, since they all roughly fall into the same story about the royalty of Thebes. However, each play was part of a separate trilogy, performed years apart. *Antigone*, despite being the last of the three plays chronologically, was written and performed first, then many years later came *Oedipus the King*, and finally, near the end of Sophocles' life, *Oedipus at Colonus*.

There is only one surviving complete satyr play, *Cyclops* by Euripides, though the three preceding tragedies are lost. Aeschylus, Sophocles, and Euripides are the three most noteworthy tragic playwrights because their works are the only plays from their time period to survive intact, though in each case we only have available to us somewhere around 10% to 15% of their full output, depending on which playwright.

We have a good sampling from Aristophanes of the comedic plays from that era, such as *Lysistrata*, *The Birds*, and *The Clouds*, though this may be because Aristophanes was born a full generation later than Euripides, who was the youngest of the three tragedians.

Greek works influenced the Roman theater, which in turn influenced the theatrical development of the rest of Europe, to varying degrees. During the Middle Ages of Europe, theater at first disappeared from mainstream society, although eventually the Church would realize its potency and return theater to a more ritualistic role in society. Liturgical dramas were used to celebrate Christianity, and proved a good tool for this and didactic purposes because most

Medieval Europeans couldn't read; books were both rare and expensive, and reading wasn't a highly necessary skill when most were farming peasants.

Liturgical dramas gave way to morality plays, which were especially popular in England, and which eventually influenced the resurgence of secular theater there. A prohibition on religious drama was instituted during the reign of Elizabeth I of England, which meant that desire for theatrical entertainment would have to be satisfied with secular drama. At the same time, traveling actors became criminalized because of their association with vagrancy, so actors teamed up with nobles. In essence, the actors would on paper become members of the noble's household, and thereby, were no longer vagrants. This is why Shakespeare's company was called the Lord Chamberlain's Men. (When James I, Elizabeth's successor, sponsored them, they became the King's Men.)

Actors also began to invest in the creation of permanent theaters. The first to be built in England was the Red Lion, followed by the creatively-titled "The Theatre," and then, the Globe, owned by the Lord Chamberlain's Men.

Theater then became a lot like what the film industry and movie-theater experience would become centuries later. Theater was not high art at the time. People often had a choice between going to the theater to see a play, or going next door to watch bear-baiting. What is bear-baiting, you ask? Well, it's a pleasant little diversion where a bear would be chained to a post and dogs would be sent to attack it, and the intrigue was in which side would win. This was on the same level as theater.

While people of all classes viewed theatrical entertainments, it was pedestrian. (Oh, by the way, Queen Elizabeth I never went to the theater. Acting companies, including the Lord Chamberlain's Men, would come to her, at court, and perform. There's a tradition that says that Shakespeare's *The Merry Wives of Windsor* was written because the Queen wanted to see the character John Falstaff, of the *Henry IV* plays, fall in love.)

At the same time, you had this newly-educated class of people who were skilled writers but didn't have anywhere to apply their skills. Playwrights like Christopher Marlowe, Robert Greene, and George Peele, who were university-educated, turned their hand to writing for the theater. The pay wasn't great, but it allowed them a creative outlet and a way to monetize their talents.

Shakespeare, on the other hand, did not go to a university, and in fact was called an "upstart crow" by Robert Greene for trying to become a playwright like Greene and his fellow university-educated playwrights. Shakespeare did, however, have an education in Latin, grammar, logic, and rhetoric. His education likely included reading the Roman plays of Seneca and Terence (the Greek plays weren't widely available during his time), and their influence is notable on his work.

It should also be re-noted, as it already was in the chapter on genre in the first part, that "playwright" was a pejorative, and that these writers would've considered themselves poets. That's what made this respectable; they were writing spoken poetry, not merely basic prose.

The big innovation from this time period, and why it deserves mention, is the turn toward complex characterization. Beginning with Marlowe and continuing with Shakespeare, characters became more than just vehicles for poetic speech; they became defined and expressed through their speech. Shakespeare's Richard III is not just the embodiment of Vice from the morality plays, even though he is partly inspired by it; Richard is a Machiavellian tyrant whose villainy makes him both repugnant and fascinating, like modern TV antiheroes such as Tony Soprano from *The Sopranos*, Walter White from *Breaking Bad*, and Don Draper from *Mad Men*.

I am an unabashed fan of Shakespearean drama (though, to be honest, I find very little of interest in his full-on comedies, though this does not include his late romances; I love *The Tempest*), and in some sense, I buy into this Beatlemania-like obsession with his work, called Bardolatry. This gives me blind spots regarding non-Elizabethan and non-Shakespearean traditions.

For instance, around the same time as Shakespeare was writing in England, Spain was experiencing its Golden Age of Drama, led by Lope de Vega, one of the most prolific writers in the history of literature. Even Miguel de Cervantes, writer of *Don Quixote*, admired de Vega's output; these two figures are usually placed side by side as the greatest writers of Spain, Cervantes usually first, de Vega almost always following, if not first himself.

There is also a rich tradition of Sanskrit theater in India, drama in Japan, pre-colonization African rituals, and even pre-Columbian Native American traditions which resemble theater. There are whole books, many of them, which deal with the history of theater. My choices for what to focus on in this chapter are based in part, admittedly, on cultural bias, but they are also based on influence. For better or worse, our understanding of theater is indebted to the European traditions more so than any other around the world, making these understandings central to a discussion of the medium. This topic does deserve an entire, separate book about it.

There is one final figure whom I wish to discuss in this very brief and very incomplete overview of the history of theater, one to whom our modern understanding of theater is perhaps most directly indebted: Henrik Ibsen.

If you've never heard of Ibsen, that's completely understandable, despite the fact that he's the second-most-performed playwright in the world, behind our perennial Shakespeare. (I'd known of Shakespeare since I was a child, but hadn't heard of Ibsen until I was a senior in high school.) Ibsen was a Norwegian-born playwright who found most of his success in nearby Denmark. While Marlowe and Shakespeare's innovation was to create complex characterization, Ibsen's innovation was to focus his drama on the problems of real, everyday citizens, as opposed to the kings of Shakespeare. Well, it was this combined with the treatment of formerly-taboo topics such as woman-initiated divorce.

Ibsen's *A Doll House* (or *Doll's House*; it depends on your translation) follows a woman, Nora Helmer, as she slowly becomes disillusioned with her life with her husband and two children, and it ends with her husband's final tirade causing Nora to decide to leave. The play ends with the husband, Torvald, hoping she'll return, until there is a final, audible slam of the door. It is a slam which shook the theatrical world, and by extension, the entire world. To Ibsen we are indebted for the dramatic works of George Bernard Shaw, Oscar Wilde, Arthur Miller, Eugene O'Neill, and many others. Basically, the 20th-century theatrical realism tradition which began to gain traction in the late 19th-century developed from the mid-century works of Ibsen.

Today, we have a theater which is no longer tailored to the masses like in millennia past, having been eclipsed in this form by film, then television, then online entertainment. Professional theater has become a hallowed tradition, while amateur theater is something so common that most high schools have classes on it. This is where we are with theater. Where we go next is anyone's guess, though it should be the guess of wiser minds than mine.

———

Theater is about performance, about embodiment. Even actors in plays with completely unrealistic and wooden dialogue are embodying the character in the sense that they are not merely reading, but are pretending to be the person speaking the lines within the fiction of the theater. Therefore, we can define **theater** as "the performance of at least one fictional character by an actor in the same space as the audience." This same-space requirement is there to say that there must be an element of live witnessing of an event, even if the event is recorded. When I say "live witnessing," I mean that the performance is complete in that moment that the audience sees it. A film crew witnesses filmic acting, but it is capturing it on camera for the final product later. The live performance must be the final product in and of itself for it to be theater.

You may also think that theater requires more than one actor for it to be narrative, but it doesn't. You can have one actor recite a monologue, and as long as there is some change in the scene, and more than one unit of action/event, you have a story.

There is also, admittedly, a question regarding both opera and musical theater, and how they fit into this. Well, that's why I didn't mention anything about *how* the performance is conveyed. Musical theater is an easier thing to include, since it's just theater but with some musical performances thrown in; yes, sometimes you can have sung-through musicals, but it isn't common, and at that point, you're probably brushing up against the definition of opera.

So, what's opera? Well, opera is a theatrical performance where music plays the central and only role. There is no spoken dialogue. It's all sung through. Musicals are a kind of hybrid in between regular theater and opera, but even if they're sung through, musicals also tend to have an element of dance, and are about spectacle. In opera, it's all about the music, and only the music. In fact, I almost didn't include opera in here at all, and was instead going to categorize it with music in a later chapter, but as it turned out, I realized that it still fit within theater.

———

It should also be noted that both dance and mime would fall under the category of theater, because while these artforms are not as primarily narrative-based as traditional theater, they have the ability to contain narrative elements, and they do take place in the same physical space as the spectators. The reason that these aren't given as much treatment here is because traditional theater (i.e. actors performing before an audience) is more directly based in narrative, though these forms should not be discounted entirely.

———

One more note before we end this chapter: there is a difference between theater and plays. Well, actually, what I mean to say is that there is a difference between play-as-performance and play-as-script. For most of theatrical history, play scripts were nothing more than instructions for how to perform a theatrical production. As I've said before, only with Ben Jonson's publication of his plays in text form did plays begin to be seen as literature in their own right, as opposed to just notes on how to put on a theatrical production.

This chapter dealt with performance, because that's what theater is. Plays as written texts will be dealt with in their own chapter, in the written medium section, and we'll talk about how play texts straddle these worlds of performance and literature, and why they're treated differently from film scripts (a.k.a. screenplays) today.

So, without further ado, let's move on to that other realm of recorded motion: cinema.

I.5: Cinema

As stated at the end of the animation chapter, cinema is a confluence of two media, photography and theater. Photography isn't given a separate chapter in this book because the only way that photographs can be narrative is by (1) requiring knowledge outside the work itself, (2) employing some kind of continuous narration, or (3) having several photographs placed in sequential order, i.e. sequential art, sometimes more specifically photocomics. We've dealt with the latter two, and the first one is our way of distinguishing narrative from knowledge. Sure, maybe you could read a story into a face, or into the playfulness of kids at a lake, but like I said in the chapter on painting, you can't read a true narrative into a single piece without knowing something about the artist, the sitter, the time period, etc. You may have that knowledge, but it doesn't come from the work itself. It comes from knowledge you've gained outside of it.

Like with many of our media, there is no one consensus as to when the medium of cinema began, but we can group the medium with animation under a broader heading called "moving images," with the term "image" being employed as a neutral between the drawn and the photographed.

A common starting point is the photographer Eadweard Muybridge. He performed studies in depicting motion through photography, and helped settle a question Leland Stanford (founder of Stanford University) had regarding his horses. Stanford wondered if a horse always had at least one hoof on the ground or if there was a moment where all four legs were in the air. By setting up a series of cameras on a racetrack, set to trigger when the horse passed by and snagged a string, Muybridge was able to capture a series of still photographs which proved that, yes, a horse does for an instant have all legs off the ground while galloping. However, the amazing thing was that when the images were shifted through quickly, it recreated the motion of the horse. Thus, film was born.

Now, the term "film" comes from the physical thing used to record images, film. In fact, of course, the word predates the common usage now, as it was first applied to photographic film. The term "cinema" comes from a French word meaning "motion," and is related to the English words "kinetic," most closely related to the less-well-known word "kinematic." The third term most commonly used for this medium today, "movie," is a shortening of "moving pictures." A fourth term used back in the day was "motion picture," which is still used by official organizations related to the film industry. Sometimes, this was even shortened to just "the pictures," though I guarantee you'll sound like you're around 90 years old (nothing wrong with that, though) if you use that term.

The difference between the three common terms is that film/cinema is viewed as referring to "high art," whereas movie is more often viewed as something "common." It's the difference between a Best Picture winner at an awards show and the highest-grossing blockbuster of the year. Things didn't used to be this way, separated between awards movies and pedestrian movies, but it's come about.

Like with the distinction between literary and genre fiction, I find this difference to be somewhat stupid, and very snobby. In my mind, these three terms refer to the same thing, and like the literary/genre spectrum, there should also be a spectrum for judging films in the same way. So, whenever I use the term film or movie, I'm referring to the same thing, although cinema is only a name for the art form, which is why it is the title of the chapter; all three may be used to refer to the art form, though. Before we move on, we'll define this medium, using "cinema" as our referent term in the list of definitions. **Cinema** is "the usage of a sequence of photographs displayed in quick succession to create the illusion of motion and thereby tell a story." It is intentionally similar to the definition for "animation," except that we've instead employed the differentiator "photograph" as a specific image, and we've also tied cinema in with telling a story, even if, for all the media we talk about in this book, we're thinking about them as story media.

––––––––

Cinema is unique among the media we've so far discussed in that, for a long time, it was prohibitively expensive for anyone but film studios with buckets of cash to be able to afford to make films. Film stock was expensive, as were even the most basic cinema cameras, and that's not even getting into the complicated use of sound technology to make what were first known as "talkies," before talkies became the only movies made. Now, sound is an integral part of how we understand cinema.

The reason cinema is placed in the visual category, however, is not only because the visual category is the most primal, but you can have film without sound. Take away sound from all films, and you'll still be able to get a basic understanding of the story, even if intricacies like names or motivations aren't expressed visually.

Finally, and most importantly, film requires actors, whereas every other medium we've so far discussed, besides theater, does not. In fact, most media do not necessitate by their very nature collaboration, though you can find collaboration in pretty much every medium. One person can write a book, make a comic, design a video game (albeit one that doesn't look anything like a big-budget game), sing a song, etc. You can even, as I said in the last chapter, perform a monologue-based play by yourself. You can't make a film by yourself. That is, until the introduction of the tripod and then, later, back-facing camera – such as what you find on smartphones – which could theoretically allow one to make an entire film by oneself, as the sole writer, producer, director, and actor.

The first effect of this fact is that studios are going to minimize risk, because if the film flops, they lose a lot of money. If I write a book and it doesn't sell, I'm not out millions of dollars, just my time (though the publishing company, which has now grown closer to the film industry, might be). However, film studios have gone bankrupt because of film flops. This is why, when sequels proved to be an easy way to get people into the theaters, sequels became a much bigger part of the Hollywood formula.

Take the Wachowski siblings. Their film, *The Matrix*, was an original property which inspired many imitators of its style and spawned two sequels, with a third in development as I write this. At the same time, the Wachowskis' *Jupiter Ascending* was a critical and financial failure. Every time an original idea fails, Hollywood gets cold feet from backing original films, even if 175 films made for $1 million apiece is theoretically a much safer investment than making 1 film for $175 million. (This discounts how that might flood the market if all those films were made and released at once; let's assume it's gradual, over time.)

The need to deliver profits and minimize risks means that Hollywood invests in what's been proven to work, even if they don't understand *why* something worked (and very often studio executives don't).

The second effect of film necessitating collaboration is that it makes it difficult for a singular author to be identified. At first, in their early history films were seen as products, not works of art. In a 1915 United States Supreme Court decision, *Mutual Film Corp. v. Industrial Commission of Ohio*, the court unanimously held that films were a business only, and therefore were not entitled to First Amendment protections. However, in a 1952 decision, *Joseph Burstyn, Inc. v. Wilson*, the Court overturned its earlier decision, bringing about the beginning of the end of government film censorship in the United States by bringing films into the same realm as literature and visual art, thereby making them protected speech.

The increasing and changed role of cinema in society is almost certainly why the Court changed its earlier decision (along with the fact that it was a different Court in terms of the sitting justices), but it still didn't solve the problem of legitimacy. Films were still often seen as products, and the closest thing they had to authors were the corporations which funded film production and distribution.

As it became easier and easier for everyday people to make films, an idea emerged during the 1960s in France called "auteur theory." Established to contrast with what the French filmmakers viewed as the Hollywood system, this idea placed the director of the film as its author (which is "auteur" in French), seeing him (it was always a "him" then) as the driving creative force in the French mode of making films. This idea has planted itself well in film studies, and it was a way of saying that cinema could be artistic, not just commercial. There's been similar debates over comics, television, and video games.

You can decide for yourself whether or not you put any credence in auteur theory, or in the idea that films need a singular authorial voice to be artistic.

One final thing in this section: the reason Hollywood became and has until very recently been the solely dominant film production center is because, well, as it turns out, a war on one's soil isn't very good for filmmaking, and both of the world wars helped turn the burgeoning European cinematic tradition back several decades, while Hollywood was safe a continent away.

———

Another important thing to note about cinema is that, unlike a novel, it isn't tied to length. You can have a film of only fifteen minutes, and while it's a short film, it's still considered a film. An analogous short story isn't called a "short novel." This makes it easier to think of the medium as a unified entity, rather than as made up of separate-length types of stories.

Short films, however, don't receive the recognition that feature-length films do, and are not therefore analogous to short stories. Part of the problem is cost. As I said before, writing a book costs me nothing, nor does writing a short story. I don't have to wrangle actors, camera operators, sound techs, shooting locations, transportation, and schedules.

Filmmakers, however, definitely have to do that. During college, I was involved with a filmmaking club, and while I (regrettably) never made a film, I worked on about seven or eight student short films that my fellow club members made. It's difficult to do all of that, and one of the biggest reasons we were able to make them is because (1) we didn't have to worry about full-time work, since we were all college students, and (2) we weren't making a work for commercial purposes. We were making something we believed in, and what we wanted to make, and maybe some of them would be sent to festivals, and would win prizes. (In fact, one of my best friends won a festival with a film I worked on with him, and he got a GoPro camera out of it.)

Anyway, the fact that films cost a lot to make is what disincentivizes short films from getting mainstream attention. Sure, you can just take some footage with your smartphone or with a very cheap camera and put it together, but it's *not* going to look like cinema as most people know it. Cinema as most people know it is made with budgets in the millions of dollars, usually in the tens of millions for ones that get awards recognition, and the hundreds of millions for contemporary blockbusters.

The difference between a movie and a painting is the same as the difference between non-comics sequential art and comics: mass-reproducibility. One of the best and most miraculous things about mass reproduction is that a copy of a work which cost hundreds of millions of dollars to make can be yours for approximately 0.001% (assuming the movie was made for $200 million and a copy costs $20, whether that be a theater ticket or an at-home, actual copy that you own). Think about that for a moment.

This means that movies have to, as I've also already said, make sure they make their money back, and that means sticking to the brand of what they're known for, which is movies between about 90 and 120 minutes (a.k.a. an hour-and-a-half and two hours). Making short films for theatrical distribution doesn't make sense from the studio's point-of-view, nor does it make sense from the theater's point-of-view regarding how you schedule theater times. Finally, it doesn't make sense from a consumer's point-of-view, because you're probably spending some amount of money and time to go to the theater and buy a ticket and then wait for the movie. You want that all to be worth everything you're spending.

Our current paradigm wasn't always the case, however. Back in the day, you'd often have short films playing alongside longer films, and at one point times for films weren't scheduled so much as you just paid your money and dropped in for a show. This time period of early cinema also had what was called the **serial film**, which was like a modern television series (remember, rhythm of delivery). The film would be shown in installments, usually changing to the next one every week, and you'd have to keep coming regularly to keep up with the storyline. The earliest instances of Batman and Superman on screen were on serial films. What killed this phenomenon? A changing market, caused in large part but not wholly by the advent of television.

Short films went away for a while, but as cameras got cheaper, they became like what they were for my filmmaking club: a way for novice, aspiring filmmakers to practice their craft with the equipment they had. Short films were cheaper and quicker to make. This independent spirit forms in part what became the soul of short-film festivals down to the present day. (Animated short films played at the beginning of animated movies are also how studios like Pixar train their new animators, whereas the old way of doing it with 2D animation at Disney was having new animators work on direct-to-video sequels.)

However, short films didn't make a mainstream comeback until the advent of home video, specifically DVDs. With DVDs came bonus features, such as blooper reels and never-before-seen footage, that could be included on DVDs thanks to the higher storage space as well as the easy maneuverability for the consumer compared to VHS tapes. Companies wanting to incentivize purchase would include these features as a way to both justify a higher price as well as promise the consumer something they could only get with the DVD.

With DVDs came the possibility of shorter narrative experiences, such as a short adventure of a side character from the main film. Often, this was on kids' or family movies. However, a notable exception comes from the Marvel Cinematic Universe.

Seeking to do some worldbuilding while at the same time incentivizing DVD purchases, Marvel Studios created five short films, which they called "One Shots," to be released on the DVDs of *Thor* (2011), *Captain America: The First Avenger* (2011), *The Avengers* (2012), *Iron Man 3* (2013) and *Thor: The Dark World* (2013). They were cheap and easy to make, with small casts and budgets. At the same time, it provided some unique ways of expanding the world of the connected universe that was the MCU. One, focusing on the character of Agent Carter, eventually inspired its own (albeit short-lived) TV series.

———

So, what importance does film have for the modern world, where TV and, more recently, online videos have taken a chunk out of audience attention and time? Well, for some, it means that cinema has begun to join theater and the novel in the hallowed halls of "high art." Watching films becomes, then, a kind of rebellion against these newer media. However, I think cinema still holds a valuable place in contemporary culture, aside from its impact on subsequent narrative media of TV and video.

Cinema and TV have admittedly begun to converge, thanks to streaming services where you can find both right next to each other. Television has become more cinematic, film more televisual in its reliance on ongoing storylines through sequels and spin-offs. Yet, film deserves to be separated from television not only because of historical differences, but because of its ability to bring us together.

Although I started this book long before the COVID-19 pandemic began, I've written most of it during the free time I've perversely been privileged to have because of the outbreak, and it's made me miss some things about how the world used to be, as I'm sure it has and will continue to do so for others. I didn't intend for this book to have any contemporary references which would date it, because most of what's in here is meant to be timeless. However, this is a useful demonstration of why I think film is important.

Film is unifying. While we stay at home and watch television and videos separately or with family, we go to theaters to watch movies. Even though theaters seem to be going away, and the pandemic has probably accelerated that trend, there is something powerful about being together in person to experience a story, on a big screen. Cinema is about reflecting ourselves back at us together, as we gather in front of this contemporary campfire to watch as flickering flames bring fictional beings to life.

Cinema, better than any medium before it, reflects who we are and what our lives are like. While TV has blurred the lines between it and cinema, this original power is still worth noting, and still worth thinking about.

I.6: Television

So, let's just get it right out of the way: the only difference between film and television today is rhythm of delivery. A film comes to you in one part as a whole work, while a television show comes in parts. What separates a television series from a serialized film is that, well, TV is not shown in theaters, and it is broken up further into seasons, with their own focus, usually. Let's just say, for simplicity's sake, that it's about platform (a television set or online) and the serialized rhythm of delivery.

When we say "television" in this book, like when we say "novel," we aren't referring to a physical thing, but to an idea. A television set is a platform for you to watch TV, even if it's the most advanced television ever. However, "television" is a narrative medium defined not by platform, but by unique conventions. After all, if it were tied solely to a platform, then there is no television on any streaming services, nor could an e-book or an audiobook ever be called a novel, even if the works within are the same.

So, **television** as a narrative medium is "a sequence of animated or photographic images which create the illusion of motion and whose narratives are both serialized and transmitted to individuals separately." As always, it's a lot, so we'll take it one step at a time and then get into the specifics.

The first part of the definition is a rehash of the definitions of animation and film, recognizing that television has live-action, animated, and hybrid shows. What's important is that, like animation and cinema, there is an illusion of motion.

The second part of the definition is the rhythm of delivery. Television has sequential chunks of story that it delivers with some separation, which, as we previously established, is a process called serialization. Even if you binge-watch a television show, each episode still has a beginning, middle, and end. Those narrative units could be just episodes, as in a TV miniseries which de facto only has one season, or episodes *and* seasons.

The third part of the definition is what we haven't really talked about yet, and part of this is because, like film, television is a combination of two previous media, though we haven't talked about one of them yet. Want to guess it?

Television is a combination of film/animation and... radio. We haven't talked about radio yet, but rest assured, we will. Early television was, in essence, visual radio, broadcasting images, not just sound, straight into homes and offices. In fact, radio only had a very short time of prominence as a narrative medium in the United States (it's different in other countries) in part because of television. Radio became focused almost solely on music, and later, talk radio joined music. Radio in the United States, however, has never really regained its narrative beginnings.

However, I anticipate that you might say that's all well and good, but what about cable TV, satellite TV, and streaming services? Those don't come from radio. You're right, but the definition of TV comes from its development as a broadcasting medium, and the first narrative TV shows were on broadcast TV. Therefore, narrative television began with broadcasting. We define the subsequent types of television not, however, by their own intrinsic properties, but by the fact that they are descendants of broadcast TV. The radio origins are still in its DNA.

At the same time, TV – just like all other narrative media – has been transformed by the Internet, and streaming services exist entirely thanks to it. TV is no longer about broadcasting, even if, as I write this, broadcast channels still exist.

This is why we defined TV not in relation to wirelessness – which, to be honest, I was initially trying to do when attempting to come up with a definition – but to being broadcast to people individually. Cable TV is by definition not wireless, as in its original form it relied on cords for transmission, as opposed to broadcast TV, which, well, broadcasts using airwaves. This is of course why the phrase "cutting the cord" is used when talking about people getting rid of their cable bundles and solely paying for streaming services.

All TV, however, is defined by being sent to individual units, whether that be to households or individual people. This is the DNA that has always remained with TV, and which can be traced back to radio.

––––––

We already talked about seriality in Part 1, with the chapter on structure, and that covers how this distinction, employing rhythm-of-delivery analysis, helps us still understand the difference between the two. I won't go over that once again, but will instead refer you back there, specifically to the discussion of the Marvel Cinematic Universe.

––––––

Finally, we can talk about the history of television, and get into the more unique elements of it as a narrative medium.

So, television at first copied radio and, surprisingly, theater, in that television at first had to be shown live. With the advent of its recording technology, however, shows could be filmed and then broadcast with edits. This is the beginning of television and cinema's confluence.

Television also encouraged the establishment of formulas; for instance, the traditional sitcom came into its formula with *I Love Lucy*. *Lucy*'s conventions would carry on for many decades, all the way up to sitcoms like *Two and a Half Men* and *The Big Bang Theory*. These are called multicamera sitcoms, because three cameras are set up to simultaneously record, allowing for editors to cut between different shots in the editing room. It provided editorial freedom.

The other notable aspect of these early sitcoms was a laugh track, which was also created under the influence of cinema. It was thought that since people were so used to laughing with others in a theater at movies and plays, this feeling should be recreated with television, hence the laugh track. It's only been that with the beginning of the 21st century, with shows such as *Arrested Development*, *The Office* (U.S. version), and *30 Rock*, that a new format emerged, one without laugh tracks or stationary cameras. This is the single-camera setup, which allows for more freedom on set for what gets shown to the audience.

While TV in Britain was, like radio, under the purview of the government and funded through a fee paid when one purchased a television, TV in America, like radio, became the domain of private business. However, instead of having consumers pay directly for broadcast TV, like they would if they went to a theater to see a film, TV instead funded itself using the model newspapers had been using for a century: advertising.

The practical implications of this dependence, for better or worse (and I'm not making a judgment either way), were that shows were written around ads. In a sense, the ads were the focus, and the consumer was the product being sold to the advertisers. TV shows were interludes from the ads, to keep viewers watching. Keeping people coming back to the same show every week, like in radio, meant that the serial format became the norm. Made-for-television films didn't become the focus for this very reason: having an end to the story meant you'd have to re-hook viewers for a new one. In film, traditionally, this was done with advertisements, including trailers, but now it's done the same way as TV: sequels.

The combination of advertising TV and the rigid scheduling of programs also meant that narrative shows were broken up into specific chunks of time. The half-hour sitcom, about 22 minutes, allowed for 8 minutes of ads, broken up into two sets of four minutes or four sets of two minutes. The hour-long drama, approximately 44 minutes, scaled appropriately. In hour-long dramas, this format led to a unique, four-act structure set-up.

Cable TV continued this trend, but it also allowed for less regulated programming because it wasn't transmitted on public airwaves, like broadcast TV was. The big advantage of cable was, instead, specialized programming. As opposed to having a Sunday-morning cartoons block, you had entire channels which could be dedicated to that and other types of children-focused programming, like Nickelodeon, Disney Channel, and Cartoon Network. This was the same with news, sports, documentary, and reality programs. Each could now have their own channel, or, as was nearly always the case, channels. We could perhaps appropriately label these "genre channels."

The drastic change, however, came with paid television, such as HBO. Paid television was the first liberation of televised content from advertising, meaning that shows on HBO could be structured differently. Instead of the ad breaks, all HBO needed to do was use the time at the end of their programs to advertise other programs, the goal being to keep people buying. (This is reminiscent of how YouTube uses algorithms to encourage viewers to stay on the platform by recommending videos they're more likely to click on.)

HBO's *The Sopranos* is often brought up as the start of the Golden Age of Prestige Drama shows on TV, and to an extent, I agree. As cinema became more blockbuster-focused, television began to attract talented individuals who were given a freer story playground, as well as much longer time to develop characters. *This* was the visual equivalent to the novel, it seemed.

HBO's influence with *The Sopranos* and other shows led back to cable investing in its own big shows, with AMC being a notable standout with *Mad*

Men and *Breaking Bad*. TV was experimenting, finding new ways to tell stories.

Then, streaming services came along. *Breaking Bad*'s placement on Netflix is notable because it became one of the first big shows to be binge-watched, creating a new phenomenon. Netflix, with its massive amount of user data, realized that there could be a show which could slot on into their content to fit this demand. The show they commissioned was based on a British television series of the same name about a conniving politician: *House of Cards*. (Despite what later came out about its main star, revelations which therefore made that show unwatchable for me beyond that point, that doesn't take away from its groundbreaking nature.)

Unlike other venues, where shows were released weekly, *House of Cards* was released at once, and was structured to be binged. No commercial breaks meant that you watched it in the same way, with the same pace, that you watched a film, while having the entire season available at once meant you could watch each season as a singular work right away, with the "episode" being a somewhat atavistic feature that was only there, really, to give you the viewer potential narrative breaks. But you could decide for yourself where and when you wanted to take those breaks.

Netflix's actions kicked off an explosion of streaming-service-original content, and also ignited what has frequently been called, in media circles, the Streaming Wars, as content providers compete with each other by producing unimaginably prolific amounts of content, original movies and TV shows alike. They also began to compete in the distribution of content that they didn't commission, buying movies from film festivals and buying distribution rights to overseas shows.

———

TV is no doubt evolving and will continue to evolve as long as it exists. What it has retained through all of its transformations, however, is the focus on seriality and on distribution to separate units of people, though admittedly now it seems that cinema is going the latter way, as well.

Television has been both heralded and hated throughout its history, but this book isn't about upholding or denigrating any medium. Rather, this book is about recognizing that these media exist, categorizing them for purposes of understanding, and then taking a look at each one to delve into and understand its uniqueness as it relates to narrative.

There is one final component of visual media which has arisen since television, one which has visual media entirely: video.

I.7: Video

So, wait, what's the difference between video and, say, film, or animation, or even television? Aren't those kind of all video? Well, what's the difference between video and film (i.e. the platform of film, not the medium)? That'll tell us something.

All right, so film is called "film" because it was traditionally recorded on film stock, though now most films are recorded digitally. Video is, definitionally, digital, but we don't say that *John Wick* is a feature-length video. We say that it's a film. So, even though the difference is in part technological, it isn't completely that.

In fact, the way I differentiate film from all of these is by defining video by how it's recorded, why it's recorded, and by whom it's recorded. So, how is video recorded? Traditionally, video was recorded on tape, a different material than film stock, and it was widely adopted by home-distribution for its cheapness. However, its entire purpose changed with the advent of home-video cameras, introduced for consumer use.

Now, however, I want to make it clear that when I say "video" in this chapter, I'm not referring to everything that could fall under that umbrella, because by some definitions, a lot of we've already talked about could move under this category.

So, it's recorded by tape, and, later, digital cameras, but cinema is also digital. This is where we get to the "why." Whereas cinema and television are recorded for mass distribution on traditional platforms, video began to be recorded for personal, home use (remember, I'm talking about home video, not video as a format). So, instead of being meant for a wide audience, video was meant for personal use.

This ties into the third criterion, which is by whom it is recorded. Video is recorded by everyday people, whereas cinema is made with big budgets and large groups of people. At least, that's how it's traditionally been. Tradition is important here because, despite the relative democratization of technology that video brings, there is a difference between even student films and Internet video.

So, what's that difference, ultimately? Well, the Internet; specifically, video-distribution sites, whether that be sites devoted entirely to that, like YouTube, or sites which host video as part of a wider platform like Facebook, Twitter, news sites, etc. Today, video, while not the only medium of the Internet, has allowed for the explosion of content. This explosion has also led to the increasing specialization of videos, which target niche areas of interest. It allows for celebrities to communicate with fans, for fans to talk back, for celebrity to be born, and for celebrity to die. It allows for people to tell their own stories, fictional or non-fictional, through a visual medium.

Video is a "a visual medium defined by its ability to allow individuals to create narratives of their own initiative by breaking down the traditional barriers to entry." Now, this comes with an assumption: that everyone has equal access to video technology. They do not. There is still, as I write this, a large amount of societal inequality around who has access to this technology, both in creation and distribution. I do not want to make it seem as if this is unimportant. I'm also not trying to be a technology evangelist, because these platforms are owned by private corporations accountable to shareholders, not the public. Their aim is to make money, not to make the world a better place. This also shouldn't be forgotten.

Still, in concert with the Internet, video has revolutionized the creation and distribution of visual narratives in the twenty-first century. The smaller digital camera (and tripod), and then the back-facing camera on modern-day smartphones, have meant that the only person needed to record a video and to tell a narrative is the person who has the camera. The Internet means that these videos have the potential to reach a wide audience.

In this space, narrative can specialize, as I have said, and reach niche audiences. People can communicate their experiences of what their lives are like, they can educate and entertain through video. However, unlike cinema, the trend with online video has not been toward fiction nearly as much as it has been toward recording people doing everyday things, whether that be playing a video game, walking to the store, etc. Admittedly, there is almost always a fictionalized, performative aspect to these videos, but again, there is now more power to the creator. In fact, "creator" has come back into vogue as an idea in visual-content creation thanks to video and its potential.

Video is verisimilitudinous. It provides a recreation of reality without needing to hew exactly toward it. In other words, it makes you as a viewer feel as if you are watching reality unfold before your eyes. This is part of the super-narrative, the story running through all video content of its type.

Yet, as I said, it's performative. All camera-capture is. Even though we think a photograph or a video captures reality, it doesn't. It can't. It captures a specific sliver of reality, sure, but the taker had to decide where to place the camera, what to take a picture or video of, and then, if editing software is employed, how to change it intentionally after the fact. Remember the anecdote of the king's map: if a medium were able to truly capture all of reality, even all reality of a single instant, it would end up just creating reality itself. The difference between media and reality is this.

It's also what narrative has become in the twenty-first century digital-visual environment. Narratives have not disappeared, they have proliferated, recording and condensing reality at a much faster rate, along with allowing for fictional stories to be made much more easily, as well.

In fact, video is so ubiquitous, yet so differentiated, that this chapter can't really be a complete overview of the subject. What I'm trying to do with this chapter, more than any other, is to give *you* the tools to look for this yourself, because, well, if I tried to do that here, it might be the longest book ever written.

So, as we say goodbye to the realm of the visual medium (at least in terms of where this book is concerned), remember that video has, unlike anything ever before, made it widely accessible to create visual narratives of one's own. The Internet, with which video is intimately tied now, has also allowed every other medium in this section to democratize, to a degree. It's not equal to everyone, nor is it based on merit, but it is there now for more people than ever before.

Video will continue to evolve, so I hope you understand that our narrative of visual media doesn't end here. Rather, if you'll permit me to be saccharine for a moment, it continues with you.

Section II: Auditory Media

Introduction

Now, we get to the second sense: hearing. However, narrative auditory media isn't merely about hearing a noise and making a deduction about it. Not really. It's about bringing sounds together to make something that is telling a story, with cause and effect, action and reaction, this happened, so that happened. For other animals, you could argue that they have something approaching this, whether it be mating calls or acting in response to hearing a potential predator. Maybe. But, for me, sound is only concrete when you have something visual to attach it to, and this means that the visual comes before the auditory. You are allowed to agree or disagree with me as you wish on that.

We humans also have a thriving auditory culture, one which leads way back before we could write. This involved telling stories around the campfire, or singing to one another. All that's required is the capability to hear language, and the capability to understand it. Sure, perhaps today, you can have sound spelled out to you if you're deaf, or visuals described to you if you're blind, but those are different media from the primary one being dealt with. It isn't that deaf people are left out of understanding auditory culture, but it does prevent one from experiencing, as a receiver, the products of auditory culture through the auditory medium category. This is one of the reasons why sign language developed, to be able to work around this.

So, in this section, we'll deal with media involving sounds, processed by the ear. While sound is another integral part of our society today, though, there aren't that many *narrative* media which are tied solely or primarily to sound. But, without further ado, let's see (or, should I say, hear? or perhaps read, which is another thing entirely?) what this involves.

II.1: Spoken Word

For this, let's return to around the same era of the cave painters, maybe 10,000 years or more later. We don't know, because the spoken word doesn't leave traces like writing does. The spoken word lasts as long as the sound waves carrying the words exist. Because language existed for probably tens of thousands of years before writing was invented about 5,000 years ago, we also don't know when language originated. The best guesses come from looking at human remains and trying to deduce if these specimens had the physiology and the brain power to process complex language.

Therefore, we have to imagine a world where the symbols on the page have no relation to the words spoken, because the symbols don't exist yet. Think about it: despite the fact that you can completely understand what I've written here, these letters have no relationship to reality. They *correspond* to sounds, and they come together the same way sounds do, to produce meaning, but they are not that spoken language itself. You understand what these symbols mean because you've been taught their meaning, but you could understand a spoken language without ever knowing how to read.

The reason I'm emphasizing this is because all media affect the way we think and understand. A professor at my college told us about how, before computers existed, people thought of their brains not like a computer (how we often think of brains today), but like a library. Is this because brains really are more like computers, we just had to catch up technologically? Or is it because we understand abstract things like brain function using concrete metaphors like libraries and computers, and those metaphors we use change based on our lived experiences?

If in fact it's the second explanation, which I think it is, then we have to understand that, in some significant ways, our world is mentally constructed by perception, and it isn't entirely objective. (However, I'm not saying everything is subjective, either; rain exists whether your brain admits it or not, but your brain understands what rain is depending on what you know and think about the world.) But what does this have to do with stories?

Well, before there was writing, people didn't think of their brains like libraries, which obviously are a product of a literate society. Instead, they thought of the brain like a river, something you could dip into and reach for something, but which wasn't completely stationary, like a library. People's fundamental understanding of the world was very different in oral cultures from how it is now.

———

So, now let's think back to those people. They don't have to live in caves; maybe they live in huts, or stone structures. These people aren't necessarily hunter-gatherers, either. They may very well live in towns or cities, settled in one place, with a robust system of trade. Do not equate pre-literate societies with childlike primitivity.

When these people gather, around a fire or perhaps by the ocean, etc., their minds become idle. Sure, it's nice to talk to friends, but there's only so many unique things you can say about hunting, fishing, farming, what have you. So, you think. Your mind wanders. Maybe you wonder why it rained last night. Maybe you wonder how humans came to exist. Maybe you wonder *why* humans came to exist. So, you fill in the blanks. You tell stories: myths, legends, complete fabrications inspired only by your direct experience.

Eventually, storytelling becomes central to your society, so much so that people begin to specialize in telling stories. They memorize lines, going from town to town to recite these narratives, and being given some food or other item of payment in return.

This is likely the derivation of all modern myths and stories from religions which pre-date writing. The stories of the first humans, or of the beginning of the world, or of the gods' wrath, didn't start with writing; they likely existed well before that.

As always, let's go to an example.

––––––––

Despite the fact that the most famous Homer today is probably Simpson (sorry, we always have to make the Homer jokes when we get to this topic), the most influential Homer in the history of narrative is definitely the Greek poet to whom the *Iliad* and the *Odyssey*, as well as some other, minor poems, are attributed.

According to legend, Homer was blind and a bard, a word for a person who would travel from town to town telling stories. (Shakespeare's nickname of "the Bard" comes from this origin.) Homer is estimated to have lived around the 8th century. He composed the two narrative poems – often considered the start of Western literature – orally, and then, one day, someone (or, more likely, some people) wrote them down. Awesome, sounds like an interesting guy. Except... he almost certainly didn't exist.

Now, this isn't to say that there was never a blind bard named Homer who performed within living memory of those who first copied down the *Iliad* and the *Odyssey* in writing, but he definitely didn't compose the poems. Rather, saying one person "composed" the poems is incorrect regardless. First off, we know from stylistic analysis of those two poems that, if they were each composed by one person, then it was two different people.

However, these poems were certainly worked and reworked over time, as the stories were told and retold, and then passed down through generations of bards. Without writing something down, memory is tied only to the human mind, and we know from decades of research now how fragile and imprecise memory can be. Each time you recall something purely from your own memory, you are re-creating the memory to the best of your ability, but unless you have perfect recall (a rare but possible ability), you're not purely drawing something out, you're partially creating it. This is why the river metaphor works so well for pre-literate ideas of how memory and the brain function.

In order to aid in memory, though, bards developed tricks. Depending on tradition, this could be a certain meter (Shakespeare, though not composing orally, used the meter of iambic pentameter, while the *Iliad* and the *Odyssey* in the original Greek use a form called dactylic hexameter) or rhyme scheme which could aid the poet in recall. You could also have epithets attached to characters, for both rhythmic and memorial purposes, such as "cunning Odysseus" or "swift-footed Achilles." So, the written forms bear hallmarks of their oral origins for this reason.

So, like I was saying, maybe someone named Homer who was a blind bard did exist and he did recite these poems, and someone attributed the works to him and him only, but this attribution is wrong. This is another complication to the idea of the singular genius of the author, a theory which often disregards external influences. In the case of Homer, you could almost say that the Greeks as a whole were the authors of the poems. What I mean by this is to show that the oral tradition complicates our current understanding of both story stability and authorship.

———

However, it's not simply poetry and prose which fall under the oral-tradition blanket. You're engaging with the modern form of the oral tradition when you tell a story using the spoken word. Pick any example you want, and as long as it's a story told through the medium of sound in person, it falls under this category. Everything else which falls under the auditory umbrella, in fact, derives inspiration and – in a sense – origination, from this source. Our next chapter deals with what could even be called the second half of pre-literate narrative types: music.

II.2: Music

Like with the oral tradition, we don't know when music originated for humans, so I'm purely guessing by putting the oral tradition before this. Perhaps, in a sense, it seems like narrative music came second because it's an addition onto the oral tradition, though perhaps the original rhythms of oral storytelling were musical, as opposed to merely spoken. Like I said, we don't know. However, music still exists in basically the same form as it always has, which means that it can be approached from a modern standpoint in a way that the true oral tradition cannot.

What is music? I'm sure you could look in any dictionary, or go onto a search engine, and a definition could come up like that. In fact, you could do that for any of these media. Instead, though, try to come up with a definition of what music is for yourself. Think about how you might define it, and then, when you want, move on to the next section.

————

So, what did you come up with? Did it have an idea of rhythm? How about lyrics? Maybe it's tied in part to instruments? Or is it as basic as patterned sound waves?

Whatever your definition of music was, it's likely correct... for you. It almost certainly reflects your experiences and particular tastes with music. If you're someone who isn't a fan of music at all, then maybe you either had a broader view of it, or you struggled to come up with a definition. (For several years in my childhood, I listened to almost no music, until I rediscovered a love for it before entering middle school, so, it's not impossible to have little interest in music.)

However, assuming you are a fan, if you're into music that features lyrics, then you are much more likely to have included that in your definition than someone who leans more toward classical music or electronic dance music. Music, like comics, is very broad, and sometimes it's just as telling to see what you *exclude* from your definition as what you include.

My guess is that, actually, you probably had room in your definition for non-lyrical music, not only because that's regained prominence in the 21st century, but also because you know that music doesn't require lyrics. Perhaps you said it has to include instruments, although electronic music is often produced solely with computers nowadays (though I suppose in a broad sense those could also be classified as instruments).

When it comes to music, I'll admit that I bias toward a broader definition, one I hinted at when I mentioned "patterned sound waves" earlier. To me, **music** is "the patterned employment of sound waves to deliver a sensory experience to a receiver which is not solely based in words." Notice there is no mention of lyrics or of instruments, although both are used to make music; all that is required is something to produce a series of sound waves in a pattern, and someone to receive them. Notice also that I said "sensory," not "auditory," because even those who are deaf can experience the sound waves of music, through touch. I also didn't add that the sensation had to be pleasurable. You may have a very different definition, and there's nothing wrong with that. In fact, keep it in mind, as always.

———

Now, that definition is great and all, but this is a book about narrative, not media themselves. So, how does music convey a narrative? The answer, it turns out, is complicated, more so than you might even expect. But, instead of working from the ground up, we're going to be working down, from the least foundational aspects of music to the most.

We'll begin, then, with lyrical music. Now, this is simple to define, since all it involves is music with some component of singing to it. However, it isn't just singing in general, but singing with a clear meaning to it. Perhaps the words themselves are nonsense, but there must be words there for the music to be lyrical.

Lyrical music's roots go back to spoken poetry, which was originally likely performed with musical accompaniment, such as a lyre; hence, lyrics. Poetry, which will be dealt with in the next media section of this book, can in a sense be seen as written music lyrics, or lyrical music can be seen as sung poetry. Either way, the two are closely related.

In fact, when teaching the 2018 Marvel Studios film *Black Panther* as part of a student-teaching program, one of the two readings I had alongside the film was a document with two songs' lyrics on them; the songs in question were Kendrick Lamar's "Pray for Me" and Vince Staples's "Bagbak." The reason I included these two songs as readings was because they were both connected to the film in some way (the former was made for the movie, while the latter underlay the film's second trailer), and both songs felt appropriate to the class's focus, which was looking at superhero films after September 11, 2001 in light of those terrorist attacks.

The class's focus, however, isn't important. To me, the lyrics worked as a reading because, in that context, they acted like poetry. However, because they were written to be heard, not read, I also recommended that my students listen to both songs to truly experience them. I'm not alone in this sentiment, either.

When the 2016 Nobel Prize for Literature was announced, it was a bit of a shock: Bob Dylan, songwriter, had won. He was the first person to win for songwriting, previous winners having received it for work in poetry, novels, plays, short stories, screenplays, etc. or a combination of those. However one feels about the Nobel Prize or the institution which awards the prizes, Dylan's selection was a bold statement, and one that asks us to consider what falls under the category of literature, and what doesn't. I'm not exaggerating when I say that the news of his being chosen made me reconsider everything I thought I knew about literature; in fact, I might not have been so bold as to call the literary-genre fiction divide "bullshit" if not for this.

However, Dylan made an excellent point in his acceptance speech for the prize, one that echoes what I said two paragraphs before: "Our songs are alive in the land of the living. But songs are unlike literature. They're meant to be sung, not read. The words in Shakespeare's plays were meant to be acted on the stage. Just as lyrics in songs are meant to be sung, not read on a page." (Isn't it funny how it always seems to come back to Shakespeare?)

He was right. Songs are written to be heard, not read, and songwriting isn't just simply about writing lyrics. This is why music and poetry are treated separately here. It's also why our story doesn't end here.

————

So, once, an old friend and I disagreed on what came first in songs in terms of importance, lyrics or music. To her, lyrics were the more important element; she felt that she listened to songs because of them. To me, however, the non-lyrical components, came first, because I could think of many songs which had lyrics that added to the rhythm, but to which I paid no attention, and there were other songs I loved which had no lyrics at all. Music without lyrics is still music, but lyrics without music are simply poetry.

In some songs, lyrics are the most important thing for me, admittedly. I like the beat in Seeb's remix of Mike Posner's "I Took a Pill in Ibiza," but what makes it one of my favorite songs, what makes it so impactful to me, are Posner's lyrics, which critique the club life often celebrated in songs from earlier years. I listen to and care about what Posner has to say, the story of someone who got famous with an incredibly popular song (Posner's "Cooler than Me") and then had that fame go to his head. The remix's club-like beats only make it that much more haunting for me, a club hit which critiques the club lifestyle. A version without lyrics wouldn't do that. Also, yes, "I Took a Pill in Ibiza" is an example of music with narrative lyrics, and it's one of my favorite examples of that.

However, there are other songs I listen to with little regard for their lyrics, whether because I think the lyrics' meaning doesn't matter, or because I find them genuinely stupid.

An example of the former is Eric Prydz's "Every Day," an electronic-dance-music song which does have lyrics, but to me, the lyrics don't really matter, though they may very well matter to other fans of the song. I love the music itself, its pulse-pounding beat.

An example of the latter is "The Hampsterdance Song," which originated from an early Internet meme in the late 1990s. When I was in pre-school, my mom had the song on a CD of Radio Disney hits from the time, and that song was the first one on the CD. I remember dancing in the parking lot of my pre-school, with a friend of mine then, to this song. The song's lyrics are objectively really stupid, but I can't help it; between the nostalgia and a beat I somehow genuinely like (to an extent), I enjoy the song.

In both cases, however, I think the lyrics add to the overall musicality of the piece, even if I don't care about their meaning. So, lyrics don't have to be the prime component of the song; maybe they're there to add flavor to it. But, they sometimes don't have to be there at all.

Now, lyrical music obviously has narrative potential, thanks to the lyrics, but what about songs (or, maybe I should say, "musical compositions") that don't have any lyrics?

I think they definitely can be narrative, and in fact, I'd argue that all non-lyrical songs have that potential. Now, I'm not saying that these tell stories in words, with characters or most other big components we outlined in part one about narrative. *However* (I feel like I say that word a lot), let's think about what we've defined a story as: actions/events, changed dynamic, sent by a medium. Obviously, the last one's been met, but what about the first two?

Well, and I may be tipping my hand slightly toward the interactive medium, but what if we don't think about the story as an isolated experience? What I mean is, what if we include the receiver of the experience in here?

Music is inherently emotional. Its main purpose, regardless of how it's made and whether or not it has lyrics, is to produce an emotional experience for listeners. In many songs, you as a listener are taken for an emotional ride, with highs and/or lows, and breaks in between each peak. There's an emotional rhythm to all songs which resembles a story, with changes in dynamics. So, in a sense, then, you're both the character and the receiver. But you are getting an experience.

In fact, going off of this, we could say that a lot, though not all, of stories told in words or with visuals are meant to provide an emotional experience. Well, actually, I'd argue that all *good* stories provide some emotional experience, but since we're not making value judgments here, and also because even bad stories are still stories, this isn't going to change our definition of what a narrative is.

I think all compositions, going back to the very beginning of music, have the potential for narrative, either directly through their lyrics, or more subtly, through the emotional experience that non-lyrical music can still provide. In some cases, the two components work in tandem.

So, if there's one thing you remember about music, it's that you can still tell a story within this medium even if you don't speak or record a single word.

II.3: Radio

So, it may seem like a natural fit to go from music to radio, as − in the United States, at least − radio is associated with music more than anything else, with talk radio coming in second place. However, as we just covered music and its narrative potential in the last chapter, this one won't be focused on that. Rather, it will be focused on radio as a unique narrative medium. Remember, the medium has to be indivisible from its content, and this isn't the case with music on the radio, though it is for what we're going to talk about here.

Radio is a potent medium for disseminating information, and no one understood that better than President Franklin Delano Roosevelt. Whereas John F. Kennedy used television to connect with viewers, and political figures today use social-media platforms like Twitter to communicate, Roosevelt pioneered the use of a mass medium to connect with constituents both directly and immediately. Newspapers had been the way that speeches and debates were sent to constituents in the 19th century, but these were delayed, and written. With radio, you could hear the president talking in real time, his voice coming straight into your home. Because this was before television, this was incredibly novel, and therefore impactful. He felt both personal and personable.

Television and the Internet have taken radio off of its peg of prominence for mass-media narrative experiences, and terrestrial radio today (as opposed to satellite radio or Internet radio) is relegated to being focused on music, although some political commentators do still use it to communicate to listeners, as well. However, before television came along, radio thrived as a medium for stories.

One of the best examples of this is the origin of the soap opera, which happened not on television, but on radio. Soap operas on radio were targeted mainly at women, who, traditionally, were expected to be home during the day. Therefore, soap operas were structured around their schedules, and were made so that you could miss an episode or two (or perhaps more) and, since the plot progressed very slowly, you as a listener wouldn't have missed much. These programs were also melodramatic, no doubt also informed by beliefs about women's interests at the time. The reason they were called "soap operas," in fact, was also related to the demographic: as the audience was assumed to be entirely housewives, soap manufacturers often sponsored the shows.

In the United Kingdom, as a sidenote, where radio is publicly owned, radio dramas still actually exist in non-niche formats, unlike in the United States. Whether that's due to the difference in ownership of stations, culture, or something else, I don't know.

But, we have to define radio before we talk about its conventions. So, **radio**, in a sense beyond narrative, is "a medium wherein which sound waves transmit information widely, to individual receivers." The reason this definition isn't narrative-focused, like the one for television (and television is, in a sense, visual radio, at least when it comes to broadcast TV), is because narrative, as previously said, isn't tied in with radio as directly as it is with television. We need to understand radio as a medium, without regard to narrative.

Now, the definition we're working with is meant to be inclusive of satellite and Internet radio, not just broadcast (a.k.a. terrestrial) radio. The key unifying elements of radio are that it is transmitted by sound, and they are transmitted to people individually, like television, whereas films shown in theaters are shown to everyone in one place. However, since the next chapter deals with podcasts as a separate subject, it may be important to distinguish these two things now, because I anticipate that the definition needs some slight refining.

First, radio is about the recording going out live, in some way. So, for instance, in both terrestrial and satellite radio, even if shows have been previously recorded, they are being sent to everyone, at the same time. No matter where you are, if you can tune into the same station, you'll hear the same thing, quality potentially varying.

On the other hand, podcasts are recorded, and are left there for you to listen to at your leisure, online. So, online radio is radio done using the Internet, while podcasts and non-radio audio in general is recorded sound which is not heard at the same time by everyone. This is why audiobooks don't fall under the category of radio, and instead would, if anything, be placed under the podcast category: they are pre-recorded, and can be listened to whenever each person wants.

So, the good news is that the definition needs only one word of a tweak: let's add "simultaneously" to the end, so that the definition now reads "a medium wherein which sound waves transmit information widely, to individual receivers simultaneously." There we go.

––––––

Despite the fact that I've separated radio and podcasts based on simultaneity of transmission, traditional radio dramas are a lot like audiobooks and animated media, in a way. In fact, another word for a radio drama is a "radio play," hinting at a theatrical legacy in these works. This is very appropriate.

Whether the actors are recorded and then their performances are spliced together, or they perform live, what happens is actors read from a script, and they, to the best ability, act out a character through their voice. Sometimes, however, narration will be employed to connect everything. Orson Welles's famous *War of the Worlds* broadcast is an example of a radio drama.

Now, note that when I say actors are recorded, I don't mean that the performance is recorded to be listened to by viewers at their discretion. What I mean is that the performances themselves are recorded. Even so, though, if the final, edited bits are broadcast simultaneously, it still qualifies as radio. The performances don't have to be live, but the broadcast does.

Because of this, radio drama is heavily focused on scripts, making it very akin to theater, and also being very similar in production to how animated movies and TV shows are recorded. No animated shows are broadcast with the actors performing live on TV, though sometimes at conventions actors will do a live reading of a script. This is tot radio, though, since the live transmission is in one location, to everyone. It would only be radio if it were sent out to listeners live through in some way.

Radio dramas do not, however, have to be the only narrative-focused expression of radio. If you've ever listened to shows such as *This American Life* or National Public Radio (in the United States), you've heard non-fiction stories covering real people, whether that be something as simple as a banana stand in Newport Beach or something as important as political activism. These are all stories, telling you, the listener, about the experiences of the people in the piece, with actions and events spiraling together to convey an emotional experience to you (or, at least, that's the hope).

———

Like any other medium, radio, as well as podcasting, has the potential to have a real impact, but unlike media such as cinema and television, radio only has one method of conveying its message: sound. Whereas film and television can use sound and even the written word to underscore their visual language, radio has sound and sound alone. This means that, well, a lot is riding on the sound.

In one sense, this is good, because it allows for more focus in one area, and it also means you need less people to make a good product. However, that also means that you have to really know what you're doing with sound. You have to know how to convey tone, atmosphere, and character without having the ability to show any of that visually. How do you convey character emotion without the face, the most communicative feature of the human body?

As it turns out, you've got to get creative. You have to make sure that the people you interview speak clearly, or that the actors you hire know how to be expressive with just their voice, but you also have to know how to write dialogue that can pull double or triple weight, whether you're doing non-fiction or fiction. Dialogue, which includes narration, is what brings the piece together, what fills in the gaps that can't be conveyed by the voices of your characters (and characters, in this sense, can include real people, of course). Whether you hire some professional to do it for you or you take on the task yourself, understand the importance that this aspect will play overall.

————

Needless to say, these rules apply to satellite and Internet radio, as well, the only differences being that you can tackle more risqué things on those platforms than you can with terrestrial radio, which is still heavily regulated regarding content.

The last and most important thing to remember about radio is that, because everyone hears it at once, it is simultaneously separating (as people hear it in different locations) as well as unifying (because everyone hears it at the same time). Because of this, radio is the first narrative technology that brought us closer to the concept of a "global village," discussed by Marshall McLuhan in *Understanding Media*. All media have a unifying potential, but radio, like television and the Internet, represents the unifying potential of simultaneous experience in a wide swath of people and areas.

II.4: Podcasting

So, to reiterate what we said in the last chapter, the difference between radio and podcasting is that radio is sent out simultaneously, while podcasts and similar types of online audio are able to be listened to whenever one pleases. A radio broadcast morphs from radio into online audio when it becomes available online for listening at any time.

So, what does it mean for something to be a podcast? Well, a **podcast** is "a digital recording of audio which is posted online for receivers to listen to whenever they please." As I said before, we're going to use the term alongside "online audio," with the only real difference between the two being that when we think of podcasts, we think of intentional collections of audio, whereas online audio isn't always that. Still, however, for sake of simplicity, I'll be using "podcast" to encompass all of this.

Because the entire idea of podcasting is tied in with the Internet, podcasts cannot come into play without the online space which, at the time of writing, has become a ubiquitous part of life for many countries around the world. The term's origin comes from a combination of the terms "iPod," the first version of which was released in 2001, and "broadcast," and it was coined to describe a new type of audio experience made possible by advances in communications technology.

The podcast quickly developed conventions similar to radio, not only because it was an audio-only format, but also because, like with radio, it was a form of mass media. In fact, most common types of podcasts, whether they be interview-based, news-based, or documentary-based, take inspiration from the preceding medium of radio, though developments in cinema and television have also played a role in influencing the kind of content that most often appears in podcasts. Due to much-lower barriers to entry required of podcasting as compared to radio, TV, film, and even online video (having visuals requires a lot more work in both recording and editing), podcasting proliferated, as well as diversified to serve niche audiences.

This is all well and good, but like with nearly any other medium we've discussed, podcasting doesn't necessarily involve narrative, though it's much more likely to include it than radio. Why? Well, as said in the last chapter, radio has become more and more focused on playing music, as TV and the Internet have taken over the non-music roles. There are websites which don't qualify under our definition of radio which do play music, such as iHeartRadio and Spotify, but these are the cases where the term "online audio" needs to be used. This is never narrative, as the only possible narrative aspects of it are from music, but of course, music is a different medium, and those websites are platforms. Podcast hosting locations, including Spotify and Apple Podcasts, are not themselves the medium, either, and they function like platforms. However, podcast platforms are obviously not the same thing as podcasts, the audio which they host.

So, like with narrative forms of radio, the focus is on audio, whether that be its capture, or its intentional design and manipulation (such as adding sound effects or music through software to the initial recording). Some of what we talked about regarding radio, especially how you have actors (if it's fictional) or interviewees (if it's interview-focused) speak, to say nothing of your own role, whether you're the host or just the person who puts all the audio together.

Some narrative podcasts are descendants of radio dramas, and therefore are only different in that you listen to them whenever you want. In podcast dramas, it becomes all about how you use the audio to convey the emotions of a scene, narration to tie things together (if need be), and how you tell the story using the tools we talked about in the first part of this book.

While we're on this subject, however, let's tackle audiobooks, which I mentioned in the last chapter as being, if anything, categorized under podcasts. Taking our definition of podcast, I'd say they definitely would also fall under the category. Audiobooks of fictional works are like long-form podcast dramas, in that they have characters and, often, feature voice actors performing the roles of the characters, though instead it may be that the narrator of the audiobook plays some or even all of the roles.

The only big difference is that, instead of having a script to perform, one written with the intent that it be turned into a podcast drama, the novel becomes the script; however, the novel already exists as its own separate work. Well, it does, in a way. The novel originates on a different platform, namely the book, but the non-physical, medium-based aspects of the novel are turned into the recording by, in essence, transforming the purpose of the platform, the book. Now, the novel is not meant to be read itself, but is meant to act as directions for a recording.

I'm not incredibly familiar with how audiobooks are made, and it may be that in some or all instances, a script is drawn up, and the narrator isn't just reading from the book itself, but in either case, the original work is the novel, written first with the intent to publish, then it is transformed into an audio file. The big differentiator, then, is what medium the work starts out in. Podcast dramas start as podcast dramas; audiobooks start as written works, and then are adapted into another medium, like how books are turned into movies.

Not all or even most podcasts are straight dramas or even fictional. Podcasts are probably most often known for their non-fiction examples, such as *Serial*, a true-crime podcast that in no small measure turned podcasts into the massive phenomenon they became. Like with documentaries, non-fiction books, or spoken-word stories drawn from life, these still contain narrative structure. The ones which have commercials, in fact, resemble TV shows, in how they structure their narratives around their commercial breaks.

All podcasts which seek to either inform or entertain should, in some sense, tell a story of some kind, with characters, actions and events, a certain tone or an expert balance of different tones, an understanding of the show's genre or genres, as well as grasp on whether the show is episodic or serialized.

The aptly-named *Serial*, for example, is split into seasons, and each season the show covers a different crime, with the overall plot progressing from the premiere to the finale. On the other hand, news shows such as ones hosted by *The New York Times*, change their subject matter every episode based on current news, and may even cover multiple topics in one episode (which we could call something like "semi-episodic").

Even podcasts which focus on very niche subjects – such as in-depth analysis of music lyrics or the discussion of terrible films – if made competently, have something to say, something that will interest a listener. It doesn't matter how widely known or widely accessible a podcast is; just as there are books which target very specific audiences, so too can there be podcasts that make their impact even if they get very little attention in the grand scheme of things. Narrative isn't about reach; rather, it's about communication and connection.

Podcasting's accessibility, plus the fact that people can listen to episodes well after they've been initially released, allows listeners an auditory connection to the past in the way that radio, like the spoken word, can never itself provide.

Section III: Written Media

Introduction

So, we've come to the written word, the thing that makes it possible for me to communicate all the ideas in this book to you by using symbols, which act as instructions to your brain for what sounds I would be making, if I were speaking to you in person.

Writing is something that's been around for somewhere around 5,000 years. It developed independently in a few different places, those being the Middle East, Central America, China, and India, with the invention eventually spreading to the rest of the world. In all likelihood, writing developed in part due to a need for recordkeeping. With cities having higher and higher populations, there was a need to keep track of people, food, and laws. For the first time in human history, a leader didn't know all of his (and it was nearly always a "he") subjects.

The first written symbols developed as ways of representing the objects to which they referred. The alphabetic letter "A," for instance, is a descendant of a symbol which originally developed in Mesopotamia to depict oxen, as, if you put an A on its side, it looks vaguely like an ox's head. What happened was that these symbols began to become more abstract, divorcing them from simply representing ideas, and instead, they began to represent human sounds. Put them together, and you can recreate, on a writing surface, human speech sounds.

There are many different writing systems which developed out of this, but the most-commonly known one today is the alphabet, in which the symbols stand not for ideas or for whole words, but for individual sounds. Instead of having to memorize hundreds or thousands of unique characters, you only have to memorize the sounds each letter makes, and understand how they work together. Any language can therefore be represented through the alphabet, not just the languages for which it was initially developed.

The alphabet's history traces back to Mesopotamian symbols called cuneiform, which likely influenced Egyptian hieroglyphs, which in turn influenced a seafaring people called the Phoenicians (the word "phonetic" is derived from the name for them), who developed a kind of alphabetic system. The Phoenicians' system was adopted and changed by the Greeks into a true alphabet, and this in turn would influence the Latin alphabet, which would be adopted by Germanic languages as well as further develop in Romance languages. Even though some alphabets have more or fewer characters than others, the function remains the same.

As we get into talking about narrative through the written word, one of the things I want to keep at the forefront is the true novelty of the written word. It is such a commonplace idea today to use symbols to express and convey sounds that we take it completely for granted, and we never think about how truly astonishing it is that humans have the brainpower to create and develop a system of abstract symbols for representing language. In fact – and perhaps I'm somewhat biased in this because I am a writer – I believe that the written word is the greatest invention humanity has ever created.

III.1: Poetry

Introduction

Because of the fact that the first oral stories were poetic of some sort, I'm putting this section first, but in reality, chronology of when each of these developed doesn't really matter, because in this one instance, the written medium itself is in a way the most important element.

Still, we're going to start with poetry. Now, our definition of **poetry** will be that it is "written, spoken, or signed work with the first focus on the language itself, rather than the information the language conveys." I include the spoken and signed word in here in an acknowledgement that poetry can be transmitted orally by spoken word or visually by sign language; however, in the context of this chapter, we're only going to be talking about written poetry.

Also, when I say that the focus is on the language itself in poetry, I'm not saying at all that there can't be a focus on the information within, nor am I saying that prose, which is the closest to the opposite of poetry, is never focused on its language. Rather, what differentiates poetry from prose is that if the focus is on meter, rhyme, layout, or just playfulness with language, among other ideas, then it falls under a poetic umbrella. Poetry is about language itself. How one constructs a poem is a central focus, and even when one completely tosses out any structure, such as in "free verse" poetry, the importance is still on the construction, since the lack of certain traditional structures is the whole point of free verse. As I've said before, even rebellion focuses on the structure against which it rebels.

In this chapter, we're going to look at different ways in which poetry is structured, and how that intersects with narrative in poetry.

Section 1: The Lyric-Narrative Divide

In poetry, there's a similar divide as there is between literary and genre fiction, although in this case it isn't about how important it is as much as it concerns the kind of things poetry is communicating. This is the lyric-narrative divide. Some poems are lyric, in that they possess a focus on a subject or an idea, whereas other poems are narrative in that they present a story.

Also like the literary-genre divide, I believe this difference is incorrect, at least inasmuch as it is treated like a binary, as opposed to a scale. To say there is a hard line between the two types is to pretend that lyric poetry can never contain narrative, and that narrative poetry can never slip away from story to indulge in flowery language for its own sake. Poetry exists on a spectrum, but these categories help us broadly classify poetry.

Also, thinking back on music for a second, lyrics in music do not always correspond to lyrical poetry. "Lyrics" in the sense of music refer to the words spoken to musical accompaniment, and all words set to music are lyrical, regardless of how little or much narrative they contain. However, lyric poetry refers to poems less focused on events and more focused on an idea or subject.

If you write a poem about someone you find attractive, but one that doesn't recount anything aside from their features and why they are attractive, then you have written a purely lyric poem. Examples of this sort of poetry are Shakespeare's sonnets, Percy Shelley's "Ode to the West Wind," and modern-day music where the singer praises someone they find attractive (fill in your own examples here).

If, on the other hand, you write a poem which details events at the end of the Trojan War (the *Iliad*), the wanderings of a Trojan who fled after that war (the *Aeneid*), or someone's spiritual journey from the depths of Hell to the highs of Heaven (*The Divine Comedy*), then you have a narrative poem on your hands. Narrative poetry does exactly what its name says it does: it tells a story. Ballads and folk songs recounting the heroic deeds of folk heroes would also fall under this category, at least if they were written down. Shakespeare wrote two narrative poems, *Venus and Adonis* and *The Rape of Lucrece*, although they're some of his least-known works.

If you want to be strict about this divide, then you have to ask yourself if the poem focuses more on the subject/idea or instead on the events it depicts. Almost always, poetry will lean one way or the other, even if it mixes elements from these two types of poetry.

Section 2: Poetic Structure

Once you know if your poem is lyrical, narrative, or in-between, the next step is understanding the structure that a poem takes. What are the components of a poem's structure? Well, the two main components are the poem's *rhythm* and *layout*.

Subsection 2.1: Rhythm

With rhythm, you're dealing with aspects of the language itself, the two most common sub-aspects being about meter and rhyme.

Meter, as we've said in the chapter on the spoken word, is about how the words fit together into a line. So, for instance, Shakespeare used iambic pentameter, an example of which is the famous line "Shall I compare thee to a summer's day?" from Sonnet 18 (he never titled his sonnets, so they're known by numbers). Now, to understand what "iambic pentameter" means, we have to break that down into those two words. An "iamb" is a specific type of what's called a "foot," or a unit of poetry. An iamb has an unstressed syllable, followed by a stressed syllable, so the way you read it is: "shall *I* com-PARE thee TO a SUM-mer's DAY?"

Below, I've written the other types of feet, whether two-syllable or three-syllable:

- Two-syllable:
    - o Dibrach: unstressed, unstressed (da da)
    - o Iamb: unstressed, stressed (da DA)
    - o Spondee: stressed, stressed (DA DA)
    - o Trochee: stressed, unstressed (DA da)
- Three-syllable:
    - o Amphibrach: unstressed, stressed, unstressed (da DA da)
    - o Anapest: unstressed, unstressed, stressed (da da DA)
    - o Anti-bacchius: stressed, stressed, unstressed (DA DA da)
    - o Bacchius: unstressed, stressed, stressed (da DA DA)
    - o Cretic: stressed, unstressed, stressed (DA da DA)
    - o Dactyl: stressed, unstressed, unstressed (DA da da)
    - o Molossus: stressed, stressed, stressed (DA DA DA)
    - o Tribrach: unstressed, unstressed, unstressed (da da da)

Some of these are more common than others, and this way of measuring poetry doesn't apply to all languages, though it does in most languages of the Indo-European family. On top of this, certain languages bias toward certain feet, with English biasing toward the iamb and Greek toward the dactyl.

Now, once you know the type of foot, you can then think about how many feet you'll have in each line. This is what "pentameter" refers to above; it means that there are five iambs in each line. If there were four iambs, it would be "iambic tetrameter" (which my personal poetry often biases toward, for some reason), and if it were three, it would be "iambic trimeter," while six would be "iambic hexameter," and so on. Greek epic poetry is traditionally written in dactylic hexameter, so six dactyls per line.

Now, the other part of poetic rhythm is rhyme, which is something that is related to the word "rhythm" in terms of the words' origins, but they mean two different things. Rhythm refers to the pattern of a poem, how it flows, while rhyme is a way to make a poem flow a certain way.

Rhyme is something most students of English learn early on. (English actually gets its love of rhyming from French, which heavily influenced English in the Late Middle Ages.) However, rhyme is deceptively simple. Some poems rhyme the first line with the second, others the first with the third and the second with the fourth, others the second with the fourth but not the first with the third, etc. There is also a very important idea called "slant rhyme," which is when something doesn't rhyme precisely, but it sounds very close. Often, this takes the form of an internal rhyme, such as rhyming "cow" with "brown." Not an exact rhyme, but close.

Rhymes can also fade away as languages change. Poems from the time of Shakespeare have words rhyming exactly with others, though those words don't rhyme together today, such as "last" and "taste." The reason we know these were rhymes is because the rhyme scheme doesn't work otherwise. This is also how we can map how words change, since rhyme necessitates a certain pronunciation, and therefore if the rhyme no longer exists, we know that at least one of the two words is pronounced differently today.

Despite how it's often taught to children, rhyme is not required for poetry. Shakespeare, my perennial example, had most of his dramatic characters speak in verse (i.e. poetic language), but very rarely did they rhyme. Unrhymed iambic pentameter became so common in his era, in fact, that it came to be called "blank verse." When poetry is neither rhymed nor has a regular meter, it's called "free verse."

There are, in fact, other ways of creating rhythm, such as alliteration (repeating sounds at the beginning of words, e.g. the 's' sounds in "Sally sells seashells,"), consonance (repeating consonant sounds within or at the end of words, e.g. the 'l' sounds in "Sally sells seashells"), and assonance (repeating vowel sounds within or at the end of words, e.g. the 'e' sounds in "Sally sells seashells").

There are even more types than that. The shorthand for thinking about rhythm is that anything that deals with how the words themselves interact falls under the rhythm category.

Subsection 2.2: Layout

Layout, in this instance, refers to what happens on the actual page. Unlike prose, in which layout is purely for purposes of printing, layout in poetry affects how one reads a poem. For instance, Emily Dickinson is well-known for her distinct use of dashes to punctuate most of her poetry, and while punctuation does fall under the category of layout, this isn't the only or even most important part of layout. Line breaks, which are when the line ends and you have to go to the next line, are a kind of punctuation, as well. As it turns out, so are stanza breaks, which are when a stanza – the poetry equivalent of a paragraph – ends.

To illustrate, take the following example:

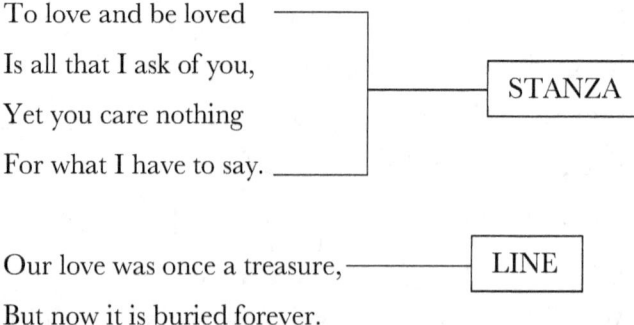

To love and be loved
Is all that I ask of you,
Yet you care nothing
For what I have to say.

STANZA

Our love was once a treasure,———— LINE
But now it is buried forever.

(I wrote that poem really quickly, so it's not the best, but it works for us.)

Now, the first four lines make up a stanza, and the fifth and sixth lines make up another stanza. When one line moves onto the next, such as from "loved" to "Is," that's a line break. From "say" to "Our" is a stanza break, with that one blank line in-between separating them and indicating that they are two stanzas.

When you're quoting a poem, you would quote it like this: "To love and be loved, / Is all that I ask of you," and if your quote runs onto the next stanza, it would look like this: "For what I have to say. // Our love was once a treasure." Great?

Yeah, well, not yet. Because depending on the number of lines, your stanzas can be called different things. A four-line stanza is called a "quatrain," a three-line stanza a "tercet," and a two-line stanza a "couplet." (Often, poets back in the day would end poems with a rhyming couplet, even if that was the only instance of a rhyme, to give the poem a sense of closure. The same thing would happen at the end of a scene of a play in Shakespeare's day, and he very often did this.) There are more, but you are free to look them up as you please. I tend to gravitate toward quatrains, but that's personal preference.

Not all poems have stanzas, also. Or, that is to say, some have no stanza breaks, so in a sense they are one stanza. Stanzas, as I said, are like paragraphs; they help organize the flow of the poem, and allow for breaks in thought. A novel-long paragraph might be an interesting experiment, but it would almost certainly not flow properly. Short poems don't need stanzas, but the longer a poem gets, the more necessary a stanza break in turn becomes. (There can definitely be exceptions, though.)

Beyond even this, though, you can get creative with how you lay out your poem. For instance, you could have two poems intertwined, but aligned at different ends of the page, therefore giving the sense that they are running in parallel. In poetry, layout affects how the reader understands the poem.

Section 3: Conclusion

Poetry is about using language itself as the focal point for expression. Out of all forms of written stories, narrative poetry is the closest we get to having the words themselves act as a character in the story, and the choice of each one plays a prime importance.

Outside of narrative, though, poetry is an acknowledgement of the power of language, of words as complex expressions that can work together to produce a truly unique experience. This has been the case since long before we began writing words down to preserve them beyond the moment they are spoken, and, I believe, it will always be the case.

III.2: Prose

Introduction

Prose is, to put it simply, everything not poetry or formatted as a script. Prose is what's more reflective of everyday speech, because almost all of us (though I admit, maybe there are a rare exceptions) don't speak in lines of poetry. We speak in words, sentence fragments, unorganized thoughts, spurts, etc. At various levels, prose is meant to reflect this. You could have prose that is well-organized, with no pauses or breaks, and which reads like it's been planned out, or you could have prose that is completely off-the-cuff, a style which often is called "stream of consciousness." Often, the latter form is found in character dialogue.

All this is to say that prose is a broad category, and beyond the bounds of narrative. Like everything else, though, we ought to ground our discussion of it with a definition. **Prose**, for our purposes, is "<u>any narrative writing whose primary focus is on neither poetic expression nor instructions for a theoretical experience in a medium other than the written one</u>." That definition isn't to say that there can't be poetic elements of language in prose, nor that prose can never be written in the form of a script, but that its *main* focus cannot be on either one of those, because then it falls into another category.

What I love about prose, however, is that it can incorporate either one of those other forms. Even more, though, what I love is that prose fiction is like a script for the reader's brain to put on its own individual film or TV show (whichever you prefer for this figurative example) in the reader's mind. Prose can still do things that are either impractical or impossible for visual, auditory, or interactive media to pull off, and because of this uniqueness to every person, is in this sense the most personal of all kinds of media.

In the follow sections, we'll cover different forms of prose narratives, going from smallest to largest. However, as a note, these categories are dealing with common types of prose-only works. Other works, such as illustrated books, which employ prose as the main element, though not the sole one, shouldn't be forgotten. Prose can be an element in many media, even if not the sole one. At the same time, we're going to focusing on prose-only to illustrate the medium.

Section 1: Short Story

Short stories don't sell the same way that longer forms of prose sell. Short stories get their attention, almost always, from being printed in one of two places: (1) an avenue specifically for publishing them on their own, such as a magazine or website, or (2) in a larger collection, either of a single author's short stories or an anthology of multiple different authors' short stories.

Despite the fact that the short story doesn't get as much exposure, however, it presents its own advantages and challenges to writers and readers alike. An advantage for writers is that the short story allows for the focus on very specific ideas, which allows for a tighter narrative than longer works. However, a tighter format means that everything is condensed, and every word a writer uses becomes inherently more valuable and costly.

However, we definitely have to define what a short story is. Before we do, something we have to recognize is that there is no hard-and-fast definition for any of the forms in this section which already exists definitively. Tying it to word count is possible, but then, all you need to do to mess with that is to go just beyond the set word count and you've now, in essence, broken the definition. This means we're going to have to define it ourselves.

Like how we defined comics and graphic novels, we should tie it into something intrinsic to the work. The only problem is, whereas a comic book is printed regularly on its own, this doesn't happen with short stories themselves as one single booklet. Many non-word-count definitions I've seen tie it to the novel, saying it's a shorter work than that. I don't like this because I think there's an in-between space between a short story and a novel, but more concerningly, it ties it to something else, rather than defining it in relation to its own qualities and those alone (i.e. intrinsically).

We know that the short story must be a complete work in and of itself, even if it may, on rare occasions, have sequels. Okay, good. Well, what does its shortened length mean for the work? Well, a tighter focus, like we said; a novel has time to focus on side-plots or go on digressions, whereas a short story doesn't really have that luxury. There has to be some streamlining of plot and characters.

There is an idea attributed to Aristotle's *Poetics* (but which was actually invented by an Italian writer a couple millennia later) of the three "classical unities," that of action, time, and place. These were originally formulated to describe theatrical works, specifically tragedies, but they're helpful to us now.

Unity of action says that a story should have one main focus/plot, unity of time says it should take place over no more than a day, and unity of place says that it should all happen in one location. I would add two more unities to this list, however: those of character and of theme. My unity of character would state that a short story should focus on either a singular main character or a small group of characters who share the main role, or else, none of them have time for characterization. If there is enough room to characterize more than that, then it's no longer a short story. My unity of theme would say that a short story should have a strong, central idea (a.k.a. theme) as its focus.

The point of all of this discussion about unities is because there is a sense that in having a tighter focus a short story is unified in its construction as well as in how the reader experiences it. Therefore, a short story will contain some, if not all, of these unities.

So, I think we have enough to make our definition: a **short story** is "a complete work of prose fiction which provides a focused, unified narrative experience to the reader." This way, we don't have to depend on binding or something like it for our definition of what a short story is.

Subsection 1.1: Flash Fiction

Although I briefly mentioned it at the beginning of the book, I want to re-mention flash fiction briefly, because flash fiction is, in essence, a short short-story. Typically, flash fiction is defined as something under 1,000 words, and it is notable chiefly because of its brevity. Because of the brevity and ease of use one finds on the Internet, flash fiction has proliferated there.

While still rarely published professionally as of this writing, it is a great way of practicing fiction writing with tight restrictions as well as incredibly quick completion.

Section 2: Between Short Story and Novel

Subsection 2.1: Novelette

This may be a new term for you, if you've never heard of a novelette before, and indeed, most people haven't. There is even a discussion regarding whether this exists at all or should fall under the second category in this section. Regardless, there is a common recognition that there is an in-between zone that exists, where works longer than a short story but shorter than a novel fall. The reason I include this as its own category is because I think there is room and need for it.

We began with the short story because we have to know its boundaries in order to understand these two subsections. The short story, then, is a measuring stick, a way of putting this all into perspective.

If a short story focuses on singular points of unity, then a novelette, because it is longer than a short story, is allowed to digress, to go beyond the bounds of all the unities mentioned in the last section. Maybe you have the points-of-view of two unrelated characters, or it takes place over a longer period of time. Maybe it focuses on two main events.

A novelette is, ideally, the length of at least two short stories, and is capable of being broken up into at least two separate sections which each have a beginning, middle, and end. Those two facts, although not hard rules, are what help signify that those unities have been broken. Even if you could read a novelette in a single sitting, you have the *opportunity* to pause between sections, because the action, the momentum of the story, breaks there, too. Remember, we measure a short story not by strict word count but by those unities, by it being quick and focused.

A **novelette**, therefore, is "a complete work of prose fiction which focuses on more than a singular experience, and which can be broken into at least two smaller, roughly equal sections of narrative." Admittedly, it could be broken down into three, but no more than four, because that becomes the domain of the next section.

Also, when I said that a novelette is ideally the length of two short stories, that was of course an estimation, because we didn't tie a short story's definition to its length. A novelette could be shorter than double the length of two ideal short stories, or longer, which is why we've tied it, like short story, to narrative divisions.

Subsection 2.2: Novella

You're more likely to have heard of this term, though still less likely than the novel. This is also the term that is often extended to include what I defined as a "novelette." A novella is essentially a mini-novel, one that is given more room to breathe than a novelette, and is thereby able to delve into characterization, digress beyond time, etc.

A novella falls, ideally, somewhere around at least four short stories, or two novelettes. Again, there is no clear delineation, and it isn't a word-for-word-count about when one changes to another. The biggest difference between a novella and a novelette is that novellas are published, albeit more rarely than novels, meaning that they can stand on their own as a work not just in terms of the story, but in terms of the product. However, of course, this last bit is just a publishing convention, not tied to intrinsic properties.

The best way to define a **novella** is as follows, from our understanding: "a complete work of prose fiction which focuses on more than a singular experience and which can be broken up into at least four smaller, roughly equal sections of narrative."

Section 3: Novel

Now, earlier, I said that a novel was a medium, and in my mind, it still is; to me, prose is less a medium than it is a medium category. If you compare a novel to a short story, there are clear differences intrinsic to these two different types of prose story that make them clearly separate, but again, this is about length, not style. Poetry is a medium to me only because there is so much variety in it when compared to prose that it seems only logical to classify it as a medium in and of itself. These differences between a medium and a medium category (or subcategory, if you want to introduce a new idea) aren't clear all the time, and this is one of these instances.

Unlike with the novelette and novella, we won't define a novel based merely on sections, although that will be a part of it. A novel is an extended work of prose fiction which is able to create realistic characters, with backstories, motivations, and, therefore, ultimately, a deep connection with its story and those who inhabit it. This is not our definition of what a novel is. This is my explanation of why I think the novel is an important component of the history of narrative in human society; it is the closest of all prose categories to re-creating the world as it is. It doesn't have to do this, but to me, a novel is at its best when it does, engaging our empathy and making us feel something deep within.

There is no upper limit on a novel, although admittedly, there was something in France in the eighteenth-century called a "novel sequence," which is analogous to a comic album in that there would be one extended work, but printed in a sequence of novels. For the most part, however, you'll find that today, a novel is a long, complete work of fiction in and of itself, though the most popular ones get sequels by popular demand.

A **novel** is "an extended, complete work of fiction, able to be split up into many individual sections of story and capable of focusing on a large or small set of characters, themes, or other narrative elements equally adeptly." In creating this definition, I tried to think of all the novels I have read over the course of my life so far, and to consider what makes them definitionally effective. Those elements, and the novel's adaptability, is what makes it a medium of its own, in my mind.

Depending on whom you ask, the first novel is the Japanese *Tale of Genji*, the Spanish *Don Quixote*, the English *Pilgrim's Progress*, or others. Depending on which era you're talking about, assuming the chapter convention exists in that era, there are a few different reasons for chapters' existence. For Dickens and those who serialized their works, it was as separate chunks of story published at different times, whereas nowadays, chapters are used to break up the story for their readers, because (1) it helps pacing, but also (2) no one expects their readers to finish an entire book in a single setting, although there are people who can do that.

Subsection 3.1: Epistolary Novel

Typically, novels are laid out in a particular way, with chapters and maybe section breaks. That's traditional, but it's not the only way in which novels can be structured. I would be remiss in here if I didn't mention the **epistolary novel**, which is "<u>a novel told through means other than straight prose, such as letters, diary entries, newspaper articles, etc., including a combination of those.</u>"

This type of novel originated using letters, which is why it's called "epistolary," the root being "epistle," another word for a letter. (If you're Christian, you may have heard of epistles by some apostles – Paul in particular – which were written in the form of letters, hence the name.) Today, however, you can find novels which do these with text messages, emails, chat logs, and other, more modern forms of communication. The intent is the same, though. Basically, as long as the novel is told mostly or entirely through means other than straight prose, it is an epistolary novel.

Section 4: Prose Nonfiction

Although prose is most often associated with fiction, the idea of narrative in neither poetic nor performance contexts can also extend to nonfiction, especially in biographies or, well, history books. History is multimedia, and has been since written history began, but history books are written, and they tell what I've previously termed the greatest story ever told. Diaries could also fall under this category, as primary-source documents (those things created by people who lived during the time in question) are a main part of what informs the historical record.

III.3: Scripts

Introduction

Although when it comes to written works, we probably associate scripts mostly with scripts for theater, the category of "scripts" goes well beyond this. When we defined what prose was, we said it was neither poetic expression nor instructions for a theoretical experience, essentially defining prose based on elimination, on what it is *not*. The good thing about this, though, is that it gives us our definition of a script already.

In the context of narrative in the written medium, a **script** is "a set of instructions for a theoretical experience in a medium other than the written one." Now, originally, after the word "theoretical" in that definition, there was only one other word: "performance." This showcases the very same bias to associate scripts with performance, as instructions for putting on a play, or capturing the story on film or in animation. All scripts are instructions, some mix of outline, planning, and mandate for how an experience will be created, but not all of these experiences are about performance. The best example of non-performative scripts is those written for comics.

There are different methods for how comics scripts are written, but all comics which have different people in the roles of writer and artist are created by the writer giving some instruction to the artist(s) about how to create this idea of a story in the visual medium of comics. There is nothing performative about this, as the script is written specifically for a completely artificial creation (assuming the comic is entirely drawn). Comics as a medium exists first in the visual category, but comics which originate with a script of some sort are in a sense made first in the written medium.

Not all scripts, though, have to be adapted into other media, and there are instances, which will be talked about in this chapter, where the script in and of itself is a literary work. That's possible, and it's been possible for millennia before Shakespeare's works were published in 1623. This is the very reason why the word "theoretical" is included in the definition; the script could *theoretically* be adapted into some other medium, even if practical concerns make it hard or even impossible to turn it into that other medium.

Section 1: Play Scripts

We've already talked about theater in this book, and I opened that chapter with this simple sentence: "Theater is performative." I opened with that exactly because of my anticipation of this chapter and of this section. Theater is the performance, while play scripts are the instructions for performance. However, not all theatrical performances are based on scripts, and at the same time, not all scripts written in the form of plays are adapted or meant to be adapted to a performance. These are different media.

The first play scripts we have come from Ancient Greece, specifically from the three playwrights we mentioned in the theater chapter: Aeschylus, Sophocles, and Euripides. Their works are the beginning not because they were the first playwrights, but because their work is the earliest *surviving*. However, unlike how plays are formatted on the page today, these works did not have **speech prefixes**, which are "the character names in scripts which precede the lines of dialogue to be spoken by the character indicated by the name." For instance, in every printed version of *Hamlet*, his famous "to be or not to be" line will look something like this, with some variation:

HAMLET: To be, or not to be

That name is a speech prefix, telling you that this line is spoken by the character of Prince Hamlet, and it is always separated from the character's speech in some way; in my case, I separated it by both the colon and the fact that the prefix is in all caps.

All scripts today will have some indication of who's speaking, as long as there are at least two characters in the script who each speak, although even a single-character play will have some mention somewhere in the script of who that single character is. It is important to note also, however, that the term "speech prefix" is usually used only when plays are printed to be read; there are more technical terms used for scripts printed as performance instructions, but we'll use "speech prefix" from here on out for our purposes.

The lack of speech prefixes in the Greek plays is due to the fact that they were originally written purely as performance instructions, and the people involved in the production would know who was speaking. This means that editors of these plays throughout history have to do some deduction with the original scripts to figure out who is speaking.

The Greek plays influenced the Roman theatrical tradition, which in turn influenced the tradition of later European theaters; English playwrights, when going to school, read and sometimes even performed plays by Roman playwrights Seneca and Terence, although as I've said, they didn't have access to as much information on the Greek works.

It should also be noted that while plays up until the nineteenth-century almost always had at least some lines in the form of poetry (a.k.a. verse), the format of these lines is still in script form, just as having prose dialogue doesn't make the plays fall under the prose category. The format of a script is different enough that it qualifies as a separate medium.

Before we move on, we'll define a **play script** as "<u>a text written in the form of a script with the intent for it to be acted on stage as a theatrical production</u>." In an opera, the scripted components are called a "libretto." In musical theater, the script is called, somewhat confusingly, the "book," although this follows from opera, since "libretto" is Italian for "little book."

Section 2: Philosophical Dialogues

In Greek philosophy, three names stand out as titans, because of their influence on subsequent thought: Socrates, Plato, and Aristotle. Aristotle was a student of Plato, who was in turn once a student of Socrates. In fact, most of what we know about Socrates comes down to us through Plato's works, so it isn't always clear what is truly Socrates and what is Socrates-as-filtered-through-Plato.

The irony of talking about Plato in regards to writing is that, based on one of his works, *Phaedrus*, Plato is believed to have been wary of the written medium, believing it was harmful because it would ruin people's memories; to him, speech was a superior form of communication. Like those who rally against all new media which gain prominence after those people have reached middle- or old-age, Plato feels that things were better in his day, that the older ways are better. As evidenced by which medium I've chosen to put these thoughts in, I think you can tell whether I agree or disagree with Plato when it comes to writing.

The other irony is that Plato railed against theater, claiming it distracted people from the real world, and said that in his ideal society, there would be no theater. The reason this is ironic is that Plato wrote many of his most influential philosophical works in the form of dialogue, i.e. discussions between characters. (*Phaedrus* is one example of Plato's dialogues.) While these aren't able to be staged as a theatrical performance, since they have no action, they could be transformed into the aural medium. You could imagine these as a conversation on a radio show, or in real life.

These works are called "Socratic dialogues" because Socrates is a main character in many of them, although his presence is not required for it to be called that. To therefore avoid any kind of confusion, I've referred to them as "philosophical dialogues." So, we can define a **philosophical dialogue** as "a discussion between two or more characters about one or more ideas, written in the form of a script, in which the intent is to come to some conclusion about the ideas through the discussion."

Although there is nothing dramatic happening in the dialogues, we still see a narrative progression, as the characters expound on ideas using what's called the "Socratic method," and then come to some conclusion. As it is both narrative and a script, it falls under our purview.

Section 3: Closet scripts

Closet scripts are the big reason why I included "theoretically" in my definition of what a script is. A **closet script** is "a text written in the form of a script and which is itself the final work, the author either unconcerned with or directly against the work being performed." The script could take the form of either an otherwise-traditional play script, a screenplay, or some other script, but the important distinction is that the script form is being used to create a work in and of itself.

The late 19th/20th-century playwright George Bernard Shaw (although he insisted on being called Bernard Shaw, editors today rarely honor this request posthumously) didn't prefer his scripts to be read or performed. Johann Wolfgang von Goethe's *Faust* and Percy Shelley's *The Cenci* were written first as literary works, though they have been performed.

The origin of this as a distinct form, however, arises around the time of

Shakespeare. As the theater was not viewed as a respectable profession, those of high standing who wrote works in script format would be confined to sharing them with friends; many of the first modern female playwrights' works were written as closet dramas (the more common term for a closet script).

Closet dramas also became popular when the regime of Oliver Cromwell, which had overthrown King Charles I in 1623, outlawed theaters and their performances. Even when the theaters reopened a couple decades later, upon the monarchy's restoration, this remained a viable outlet for some writers. Shelley's other well-known work in script format, *Prometheus Unbound*, was written with the intent to be read only, with Shelley adding elements that would make it lean toward the literary as opposed to the performative. Even Edgar Allan Poe wrote a play for literary audiences; called *Politian*, it was published in *The Southern Literary Messenger*, although poor reviews meant that Poe abandoned this work unfinished.

Although closet scripts are, strictly speaking, written with the intent first to be read, all scripts which are distributed in the written medium to be read as they are could be classified as closet scripts in the sense that the focus in these situations is on plays as literary, not performance, texts.

Section 4: Screenplays and Teleplays

In a strict sense, screenplays are instructions for the recording of a cinematic work, with the TV equivalent being called a "teleplay." We're going to define both now: a **screenplay** is "a script written as a set of instructions for the creation of a film," and a **teleplay** is "a script written as a set of instructions for the creation of an episode of a television series."

Screenplays (and teleplays) are probably the least literary of all that we've mentioned so far. The publication of film scripts is a recent phenomenon, and it's usually aimed at fans of either the film itself or of cinema in general. I do, however, recall in high school seeing a script for an episode of the original

Twilight Zone series, "The Monsters Are Due on Maple Street," in one of the big books of literature from a company called Prentice-Hall that we read from. It's rare, but it does happen.

If I had to guess as to why it is rare to treat screenplays as literary, I would say that it involves a combination of four things: (1) respectability, (2) recency, (3) technicality, and (4) pre-existing records.

(1) Films, and television even more so, are often seen as lower forms of art, if art at all, because of their mass appeal, and so are seen as less worthy of serious study, though as I write this, these beliefs have been evolving in the 21st century.

(2) The fact that films and television are more recent media is another tick against them. As previously noted, while in Shakespeare's time the theater was seen as low entertainment, now it, and the texts of the theatrical tradition, are respected. Film has a leg up on television in that it's been around longer, but it too is still mostly looked down upon.

(3) Screenplays and teleplays possess more technical language, since they are a more involved and modern process than theater is, though I would bet that modern play scripts are also technical.

When talking about a script for a film he was starring in, the actor Eddie Redmayne praised the script as reading like a novel, but in reality, that was damning, even if Redmayne thought it was the opposite. A screenplay *shouldn't* read like a novel; it isn't one, and we shouldn't view the novel as something a screenplay should aspire to emulate. A film or TV script is first and foremost a collection of instructions for performance. It serves a utilitarian purpose, and, therefore, description should serve production, not readership.

How is this third problem solved? Well, you have to make the script more literary when you print it. Perhaps you add more description of action, or the scenery. Maybe you take out the technical language of locations and instead make that descriptive. You're in a sense turning a screenplay into a kind of transcript, or recording of the film or TV episode, and you have to ask yourself if the point is to convey the original script, or the product as filmed, but either way, these are possible. This is also assuming that the intent is for the script to be read by a wide mass of people. If you expect it to be read by people more knowledgeable about film, you don't have to do this.

(4) This is the problem my English teacher taught me my senior year of high school. Basically, film and TV exist on their own, whereas the theatrical performance is re-created every time (notwithstanding recorded theatrical performances), meaning that the script is the permanent component for theater. In film and TV, the visual product is permanent, therefore the preservation and consumption of the script is unnecessary. I agree with this if we see film and TV shows only as entertainment, but if instead we treat a film or TV show as a work of art, then I think the script does deserve its own place of interest.

Now, on that note, are all or even most films and TV shows art? No, but neither are most products of any medium. Art is difficult to make, and while I'm refraining from making a value judgment here (because I find that useless for our purposes), art is rarer than entertainment because of the higher difficulty in making it. We may all have different ideas of whether something is art or entertainment, but we all, I believe, can recognize that there is a distinction, one I tried to outline in the chapter on genre in Part 1.

Section 5: Miscellany

A script can be for anything, really. As mentioned, comics have scripts (and even if a comic is created by a writer-artist, you'll almost never find someone who draws without some kind of a planning document, though it does happen), radio shows have scripts, and video games have scripts (although there is no set format for a video-game script). Even speeches can be seen as scripts, assuming the speech was written out and planned beforehand, and is then either read off a prompter or recited from memory.

You could even make the case that all written media is a script for your brain in some way, to which I alluded in the previous chapter. Although I like thinking about that, I also believe that there is an important component of written media that is purely script-based, and that component should be understood separately. Hence, this chapter.

Section IV: Interactive Media

Introduction

Interactive media is the most recent media category to develop, because it develops out of the preceding media categories, visual and written more so than auditory. In talking about interactive media, I defined it in relation to the sense of touch because interactivity involves the receiver in an active role. In fact, the defining characteristic of interactive media – and that which defines it as a separate category – is this relationship between the creator and the audience.

All media are, to some degree, interactive, though. The experience of a book or a film is not complete upon the work's creation, but upon its reception by an audience, even if the only person to experience the finished work is the creator. All works of expression, not just the narrative ones, are like a two-piece puzzle: the creator provides one piece, and the audience the other. Oftentimes with creative works, more than one piece fits in that second place, but the work is not complete without a second, audience-provided piece.

Interactive media differ, however, because they let the receiver decide on the *first* piece of the puzzle, as well, not just the second. Interactivity makes the audience member, or receiver, a co-author, allowing them to create their own experiences with the work. As long as there is some agency for the audience, as long as they get to direct a certain part of the experience, then it is interactive.

There is, however, one requirement which I am going to add on to our understanding of interactive media: a **feedback system**, which is "the way in which a piece of interactive media actively and directly responds to the user's choices, and therefore, how that piece of media qualifies as interactive in the first place." Each person must be able to have an effect on the experience *and* be able to knowingly experience the results of that effect.

As an example of what wouldn't fall under this category, we'll look at the example of TV shows, films, or theatrical performances which ask for an audience *vote* to determine which ending will be chosen. On its surface, this seems interactive, and perhaps others would say it is, but I wouldn't. Now, if you were watching the piece at home, and you got to decide which ending to watch, that would be interactive. So, what's the difference?

In the voting example, the end result is the product of collated choices leading to a single conclusion. If I vote for a different outcome than the majority did, then I have had no effect on the experience, therefore I cannot experience that effect, and therefore, to me, the experience is completely non-interactive. There may as well have been no vote at all, as to me, this is the definitive ending.

At the same time, if I voted with the majority, then I am experiencing the results of my vote, but I did not have a noticeable effect on the experience. The only possible exception is if the majority were chosen by a single vote, then in effect, everyone who voted for the majority did make a difference, since that single vote could be anyone's, and, therefore, it is everyone's.

On the other hand, if I selected the ending myself, at home, then both criteria are met, so long as I can know that for certain there are alternate possibilities. If there are two options presented, but both lead to the same result, then there is no choice, only the illusion of it, and therefore, no interactivity.

Interactive media has been around since before the advent of computers, but computer technology has facilitated the proliferation of interactive content, whether that be video games, interactive movies, or text adventures with multiple paths, among others. We will keep that in mind as we move forward.

IV.1: Non-Game Interactive Media

Introduction

In this part, media will be broken up into sections based on our previous media categories, because the big connecting thread is interactivity itself. Games will be a separate category covered in the next chapter.

Section 1: Written Media

Introduction

The ability to have interactive written experiences dates back to the beginning of the written word, though only theoretically. The advent of using the written word to provide for a choice-based experience came about with such works as the *Choose Your Own Adventure* book series, which started in the 1970s. The *CYOA* books were so influential that the phrase "choose your own adventure" is still often used to describe interactive, written stories, even as these stories have gone away from books and into digital spaces.

Subsection 1.1: Text Adventures

Beyond books, however, in the same decade came the first interactive-fiction experiences, which some would call games, though I'm reticent to use the term. These works started to come out before even computer mice were standard with computers, meaning the way to navigate them was to have typed commands pre-programmed. For instance, the player is put into a situation and given some starting description, such as the following:

> You wake up in a strange and mysterious room, lying on the floor. You rise, and the realization hits you: you need to figure out where you are, and fast.

There isn't necessarily an actual time limit; phrasing like that is often just being there to increase the drama.

You would then type in a command to move in a direction, such as "GO NORTH." Then, let's say when you went north, more text appeared, telling you that you were facing a door. If you wanted to go through, you would type "OPEN DOOR," then, if it opens, say "GO NORTH," at which point the text would tell you that you've entered a new area, and maybe describe it. You could also decide to investigate the room further, in which case you could either "GO SOUTH," then "GO WEST," or "GO SOUTHWEST."

It's clear how these would provide a narrative experience, because they work very similarly to video games, although your feedback is text-based instead of visual. Is this a game? Well, *CYOA* books were often called "gamebooks," and text adventures (which is the name of this type of interactive written media) are often called games; while I use the same terminology in real life, for clarity, I won't be calling these games. If it falls under interactive media but is not a game, then it is an "interactive experience."

A **text adventure**, by the way, is "<u>an interactive, text-based narrative which is navigated through the use of text commands typed through a keyboard into a computer</u>." Although there are programs which exist that allow you to write these, you could also simply write them within a programming language itself, and instead of creating a space to navigate, you could have people enter numbers for certain choices. (After taking an introductory course on Python, I used it for this very purpose, because at the time I hadn't learned about any other ways to make interactive text-based experiences.)

Subsection 1.2: Hyperlink Adventures

As mice became standard with computers, and as those computers became mainstream, a second type of interactive written media arose, one which is navigated not by text commands, but by using hyperlinks. Hyperlinks are links that can be clicked on, and then, once clicked, the computer is given instructions to navigate somewhere else, such as in the same space, another file on the computer, a website, etc. The most well-known piece of software, currently, which allows users to create these experiences is a program called Twine.

The big difference is, perhaps evidently, that text adventures involve typing commands, and hyperlink adventures involve clicking on links. So, a **hyperlink adventure** (which is not an official term, as far as I'm aware) is "an interactive, text-based narrative which is navigated through clicking on hyperlinks to be taken to different digital locations."

Section 2: Visual Media

Introduction

Interactive visual media became viable as a result of the development of digital technology as well as of distribution methods. Only when one could view movies or TV episodes at home could one have a truly interactive experience with visual media, because a collective viewing experience, as previously outlined, does not allow for interactivity by its very nature.

There may be a comic book with diverging storylines that one can choose to follow, and this would be interactive visual media, since comics are a visual medium. However, it is relatively rare to find this, at least in the mainstream. It is, however, a possibility.

Subsection 2.1: Movies

"Have you ever wished your favorite movie would have ended differently? Well, now, *you* can have control over the ending." This was a big selling point for the idea of interactive, at-home cinema, though that quote is my own, made only for exemplary purposes.

The development of digital video technology, such as the DVD, made it possible to skip ahead to certain sections based on player choice, which would not be possible with analog technology. A modern example of this, albeit not on DVD, is *Black Mirror: Bandersnatch*, a Netflix interactive film made by the producers of the *Black Mirror* television series and which allows for the viewer to make decisions as to how the story progresses, while also allowing them to go back and replay previous decisions.

Also, the talk of interactive movies brings into question the distinction between these and video games, because there was a type of video-game popular in the 1990s called "full-motion video," wherein the game was made up of real video footage, sometimes entirely that, but it was presented and structured like a game. While I believe that these often do qualify as games, I'm mentioning them here because of the very blurry line in this case between the two categories.

Subsection 2.2: Video

With the Internet and the ability to utilize hyperlinks in interactive media, video has become a viable outlet for interactive narratives. On YouTube, one can create links to other videos within the first video, allowing for an interactive narrative to play out much the same way as a written Twine narrative would.

Like in the non-interactive video realm, this medium takes down some of the traditional barriers to entry, and the relatively easy use of sites like YouTube adds to accessibility; as long as one has access to a camera, the Internet, and editing software (though the last is not inherently necessary), one can create interactive video-based content and allow others to experience it, across the world, as long as those others also have an Internet connection and can understand the language used in the videos.

Section 3: Auditory Media

Auditory media doesn't really present itself as a viable medium for interactive narratives, since music doesn't really present a chance for the receiver to make choices about how a song progresses, and radio is a mass medium only, therefore cannot be interactive by our definition. However, podcasting certainly could allow for choice-based narratives, and the spoken word certainly could have given audiences the opportunity to influence the storyteller's choices about where to take the story. (Though, again, a collective decision wouldn't make it interactive. An individual decision would.)

However, since there aren't that many examples of interactive auditory media, the above acknowledgement has to suffice, at least for now. Maybe one day, however, interactive auditory media will become a much more common part of the media landscape.

IV.2: Games

Introduction

Games have existed in human society for thousands of years, though that doesn't mean that it's easy to define what they are. Scholars in the field of game studies have multiple definitions about games, how games are distinct from play, and how we can differentiate games as a separate medium. We'll try to do that here.

One commonly-cited element which differentiates games from mere play is that games are structured. Games have rules and are situated within a frame of requirements, whereas play, by its very nature, is unstructured. With games, it's as important what constraints are placed on the players as what they are allowed to do. This is true whether you're talking about sports, video games, board games, or anything else.

Games are built based off of **mechanics**, which are "the base-level actions a player can take when in a structured interactive environment." For instance, a mechanic in an adventure game series like *Uncharted* is shooting, or running, or jumping, or ducking in cover. The idea of mechanics is most prevalent in video-game design, but the idea of allowances and constraints is in all games.

However, *Black Mirror: Bandersnatch* has a mechanic, in that you can click on which path you'd like to take. Why is that not a game? What makes games unique? Win states. A **win state** is "an outcome that happens once certain conditions are satisfied, and which indicates that a player has finished the game with success." A soccer game ends when the time is up, but the win state comes about by getting more points than the other team before the time runs out. A video game ends when the player completes the story missions, or, if it's in multiplayer, when one team beats the other. Non-game interactive media do not have win states, nor do any previous media categories we've discussed.

Before we go on, however, I have to acknowledge that this distinction is only being used for this book. Often, interactive experiences which are programmed like video games are called "games," and in conventional speech, this is fine. We're not saying the terminology has to change for everyday use, and that people should only adhere to exactitudes, all the time. All we're doing with this distinction is separating non-game interactive media from games so as to understand their core functions. Also, the question of what constitutes a win state may also in certain cases be murky.

Section 1: Defining Win States

However, before talking about games and their relationship to narrative, I'd like to get into a way we *can* define win states.

So, all games which have win states also contain goals. A **goal** is "a condition of a game which needs to be met in order to advance to a further stage, and, ultimately, win the game." So, goals build toward the win state, and a win state can in turn be seen as an ultimate goal; the two are fundamentally dependent on one another. Assuming there are multiple goals in a game, those goals can interact or clash with one another.

Now, the goals of a player don't necessarily need to be the same as the goals within the game, but the goals which build to win states are the ones which we're talking about here. For instance, if I'm playing a game and all I want to do is explore, rather than play through the story, then that's my goal, but not necessarily the game's. Games very often provide side content encouraging exploration, but at that point, exploration becomes an integrated goal, in that it is part of the game, rather than solely coming from the player's desires. This dichotomy of player versus game, or player in sync with game, comes about because of games' interactive nature. Games are authored (all have to be, at the basic level), but they seek to allow for a degree of choice from the player.

Many games have micro-goals and macro-goals; a micro-goal is a goal which the player has to achieve in order to progress to the next task, whereas a macro-goal is what the micro-goals are building toward. In chess, for example, capturing an opponent's piece is a micro-goal, while the macro-goal is to capture the king. A win state is therefore the ultimate macro-goal, assuming that there are smaller micro-goals which build toward it. However, a game can be made with just micro-goals, even as basic as achieving a higher score in a game with no defined end. The closest thing to a win state in that case would be getting the higher score. Therefore, the actual bounds of the win state can change in certain games.

Section 2: Games as Play or as Narrative?

There is allegedly a debate between people who see games primarily as structured-play activities ("ludologists") and people who see games as narrative ("narratologists"). The ludologists would look primarily at what we just talked about in the previous section, while the narratologists would look at how games tell stories. (We've essentially taken the narratology approach throughout this entire book with other media.) Although there is debate about whether or not this debate itself exists, I don't really think it matters whether it exists or not, because I think it brings up fascinating questions regardless, but I also think we can come to a firm conclusion about it.

I first learned about this debate from a 2002 paper called "Game Design as Narrative Architecture," written by scholar Henry Jenkins. Jenkins quotes one unnamed critic as saying "[interactivity] is almost the opposite of narrative" because narrative, in the critic's definition, is directed by an author, while interactivity is directed by the player. Even Jenkins himself agrees to an extent, saying that games are made up of more than just story. While games, like any other medium, have intrinsic qualities which are unique to it and that other media would find difficult or impossible to replicate, there seems to be this notion inherent to the debate that "story" is somehow this foreign element which is placed atop certain games, that it belongs with media which have narrative, fictional or non-fictional, as a central component (like all the other ones we've talked about). This notion is completely wrong. In fact, interactivity *is* narrative, and it fits within how, in this book, we've grown to understand what narrative is.

Our final definition of story/narrative (which are interchangeable terms for us) was "a sequence of intentionally-collected actions and/or events which each change the dynamics of their scene and which also cohere together to convey an experience through a medium to a receiver." In terms of games, let's think instead of "receiver," which is passive, that it is "participant," since interactive media is defined by participation. Now, let's return to Jenkins.

One of Jenkins' major points against the narratologists' focus is the idea that "[not] all games tell stories," with Jenkins citing examples such as "*Tetris, Blix,* [and] *Snood.*" However, Jenkins fails to consider the true meaning of narrative, and thereby exemplifies why this ludology-narratology dichotomy exists at all.

First, as I said in the last section, all games have authors, not just the ones with stories in the olden sense. A programmer who employs coding or a designer who invents a table-top-role-playing game is creating the game not by mandating a series of events to be experienced by the players, but by creating the constraints, i.e. the mechanics and rules. All mechanics are statements by the creators on what players *can* do, and all rules are statements on what the players either *must* do or must *not* do. (If a player cannot do something, it is indistinguishable from something they must not do.) Therefore, all games, going back to the first games ever played, are authored. Perhaps they're authored by tradition, perhaps they change over time, but they are still authored by those who engage in meaning making or meaning alteration with regard to games' mechanics and rules.

Second, even when restricting the idea of "authorship" to the old way of thinking about it, where authorship is about creation and interactivity is about allowance (as another part of that critic's quote claims), then this idea of certain games not having a narrative falls out the window, but this is because of a narrow definition of narrative. There is nothing in *Tetris* which conveys to a player a "story," therefore it is narrative-less. Well, assuming that part is true, what about in the interface between the game and the player? By playing the game, by making decisions of where to place blocks, are players not then *authoring* a narrative by taking actions which then convey an experience back to them and where their choices change the dynamics? As I said, it seems that interactivity is narrative.

This notion of a meta-story is in fact what makes interactivity, as seen through games, unique. It isn't that they eschew narrative entirely, but that the narratives they create exist outside of the bounds of the medium, and are created by a back-and-forth between the system and those interacting with it. This is what Jenkins and others fail to account for. In fact, by insisting on only viewing the idea of narrative through their limited lens, what they have done is contradicted themselves. "The application of film theory to games can seem heavy-handed and literal minded, often failing to recognize the profound differences between the two media," Jenkins says. However, by judging games with the same understanding that one uses with older media forms (not just film), these scholars, Jenkins included, are imposing older media understandings onto this new and different medium, in effect doing exactly what he warned against doing.

In the words of Marshall McLuhan, "the medium is the message." If we are to grasp an understanding of games, we cannot exclude an understanding of narrative from this medium because our old understandings of narrative don't fit it. As this whole book is meant to convey, narrative is a *framework* for understanding how media express meaning and convey experience. Games, on the other hand, are a medium, and while they are not immutable to change, a framework should fit the fact, not the other way around. Just as Einstein changed our understanding of gravity from Newton's original not by throwing the latter out but by broadening "gravity" to include but go beyond classical mechanics, so too should our understanding of narrative be broadened as new media emerge with their own distinct attributes to use for conveying their messages.

Section 3: Games as Play *and* as Narrative

So, the ludology and narratology approaches are completely compatible. We can look at games as telling stories through their systems, as I said in the last section. However, we can of course also look at games which tell stories through characters, the written word, dialogue, and other elements which games draw from other media. Direct narratives can also be feedback, as well.

Still, I want to emphasize the systems-based stories here, because that type of story is what's unique to games. "John Smith made a goal in the last seconds of the game, which meant his team won the championship." This is a story, with actions and dynamic-changes, which is conveyed through a medium to a receiver. For you, the medium is the written word, with no interactivity, but for John Smith, the experience was not only interactive, it was a game; as a participant, he had an effect on the outcome, and he was part of the narrative of play.

Games are a narrative form that has existed for millennia while also being very mutable, evolving more quickly and broadly than any other medium. This means we have to understand that narrative is not excluded, but broadened, by games' increasing ubiquity. Games could be the prime medium of the future, despite being very old, but they are a medium just like any other, and capable of engaging our empathy, our interest, our very selves, through narrative.

Conclusion

As media becomes more and more central to lived experiences in the world, as technology becomes more complex, and as we continue to understand ourselves and each other through media, it is imperative that we also come to understand what narrative is, what it has been, and what it could be. Long before personal computers, long before we could watch movement on screen, or hear a recorded voice, we listened to bards, we talked about our experiences, and we looked at the world and saw patterns.

No matter which human civilization you choose, no matter how far back you can look (and almost certainly beyond that), you see curiosity, engagement, and empathy. You see people looking at their world and trying to understand it, each other, and themselves. It is a universal human instinct, a language which escapes the boundaries of time and space, one that seems baked into the very fabric of who we are as human beings.

Narrative is also a powerful tool. It can be used to inspire people, to build entire civilizations, to progress society by facilitating invention. But it can just as easily be used to explain and even justify prejudice, injustice, and general harmful actions. All wars are based in the human capacity to make their side the good ones and the other side the bad ones, and wars are narratives of how humans destroy other humans. I do not judge whether wars are just, but I also am, fully honestly, no fan of war itself. The heights of human greatness, the depths of human depravity, and everything in between, all form one long, ongoing, interconnected narrative network. We try to understand this through history, through science, through mathematics, through literature, and through countless other subjects and methods, all adding to create a metaphorical map of our experiential world.

We must always remember, though, that this map, this narrative that we seek to understand, will never be complete and all-encompassing. If it were, then in reality what we would have is the world itself, re-created.

Acknowledgements

It's hard to give everyone the credit they deserve in helping with this book, or any other one, for that matter. You could very easily argue that every person a writer encounters has some impact on the thing they make, and I'm certainly no exception to that. Anything I make, I owe to everything and everyone who came before me. That being said, though, there are people who deserve specific thanks for making this book possible, in different ways.

So, thank you first and foremost to the man who started me on my path as a storyteller, my father, Al Ten. He taught me not only what a good story is, but what a good *experience* is, as well. That, to me, is what makes stories special, the experiences they give to you. He also always supported my love of the arts.

Thank you to my mother, Sharon Ten. When the COVID-19 pandemic began, I was in the midst of finishing my final year at the University of Virginia, only two months away from graduation. I'm grateful that she provided a place to stay, as well as allowed me some time to adjust to the new world. Far from everyone has the privilege that I had in that regard, and I'm grateful for that, as well as her emotional support throughout all my years of writing.

Thank you to my two-time art history teacher from high school, Mark

Davis, who was the first person outside of my family to take an active interest in my writing, as well as to encourage me in what I did. Even though I never had him for English, I definitely learned a lot about the subject (and the arts in general, of course) from him.

Thank you to Bruce Williams, my mentor in the University of Virginia's Department of Media Studies. I entered the program expecting to learn about film, but I came out of it with a much broader perspective about the world and how we humans communicate in it. While this book wouldn't be what it became without the department, however, it owes a specific debt to all the conversations he and I had over my four years during office hours.

Thank you to Sean Duncan, my second mentor in Media Studies. While I only got to know him in my final year at UVA, he taught me almost everything I know about analyzing and creating games. He also, through his comics class, introduced me to an entirely new media environment, which included Scott McCloud's *Understanding Comics*. Even though I had started the first chapter or so of this book before that class, McCloud's work, and the comics and games classes in general, influenced this book from front to back.

Thank you to Jackie Kosmacki, a filmmaking inspiration of mine and someone I'm honored to call a friend. I'm incredibly grateful for all of our in-depth conversations about film as an art form. However, her trust in my advice for her screenplays is no small part of what gave me the confidence to write this.

Thank you to Grandpa John. I'm so sad that I don't remember the few times I saw you before you passed away, but your work has still been one of my biggest inspirations for the kind of skill I want to cultivate, albeit in my writing as opposed to drawing, because I can't draw worth a cent.

Thank you to all of my students in "National Marvels: Superhero Films After 9/11." You all gave me an amazing first teaching experience, one that's made me only want to continue teaching people, in whatever form that takes, in the future, including this way.

Thank you to my friends Annelise Miranda, Anthony Malabad, Asher Caplan, Buck Schoorens, Cadesia Boulware, Elias Azar, Grace Eva Leffler, Jeff Niznik, Joel Calfee, Laura Ramirez, Layne Berry, Letti Rivas-Garcia, Marie Pinto, Martin Moro, Maura Davis, Michaela Culhane, Ruby Peters, and Will Norton. All of you have been amazing friends to me, and I'm unfathomably lucky to know all of you.

Finally, thank you to the entire Browning family. I met Dave Browning through my Cub Scouts group, but I got to really know him outside of that. He taught me so much about what it means to be a thoughtful human being, while also maintaining an inexhaustible curiosity about the world. His son, Ian, is my oldest friend, but more than that, he really is like my brother. The whole of the Browning family, in fact, feels like my own, and getting to know each and every one of them has shaped my life beyond which words can describe. Not only would I not be the writer I am today without them, but I wouldn't be the person I am today without them.

So, yeah, that's a lot of names. Like John Donne wrote, "No man is an island." We don't get where we are without others, and that's always been and always will be true of people. So thank you again to everyone I mentioned, as well as to everyone who has influenced me whom I couldn't mention in this final section, including you.

Thank you.

Glossary

Act: a division of drama which demarcates units of the story based on actions or events which change the stasis of the entire narrative.

Action: something that an agent does.

Animation: the usage of a sequence of images displayed in quick succession to create the illusion of motion, and the images are created using an artificial process.

Antagonist(s): the force(s) of opposition to the protagonist(s), not necessarily even a sentient character (e.g. weather).

Anthology: a collection of unrelated stories (or general works) whose relationship is determined by shared medium, genre, time of creation, and/or other similar trait(s).

Art vs. entertainment: "art is meant to make people inclined to forget ~~remember~~, while entertainment is meant to make people inclined to ~~remember~~ forget."

Chapter: a division in a book that separates content into sections, thereby differentiating the content in that section from what comes before and/or after it.

Character arc: the sum of experiences which a character undergoes throughout the course of the narrative which causes that character to change.

Cinema: the usage of a sequence of photographs displayed in quick succession to create the illusion of motion and thereby tell a story.

Closet script: a text written in the form of a script and which is itself the final work, the author either unconcerned with or directly against the work being performed.

Coding: Connoting ideas about characters through their external characteristics without explicitly denoting that those ideas apply to them.

Comic book: a single unit of comics content which is not spine-bound, not a complete work in and of itself, or both.

Comic strip: an ongoing comics series published in a periodical not solely devoted to comics.

Comics: mass-reproducible sequential art.

Continuous narration: a technique in the visual arts of painting, drawing, or sculpture where a single image displays several moments at once.

Deuteragonist: term for a secondary protagonist, but one who is not as central of a focus as the protagonist (hence: second*ary*, not *second* protagonist).

Episodic anthology: a television show where the cast and story change every episode.

Episodic story: a story that is told in chunks, but each chunk is distinct from the others.

Epistolary novel: a novel told through means other than straight prose, such as letters, diary entries, newspaper articles, etc., including a combination of those.

Event: something that happens to someone.

Feedback system: the way in which a piece of interactive media actively and directly responds to the user's choices, and therefore, how that piece of media qualifies as interactive in the first place.

Foil: a character introduced to contrast with the protagonist or antagonist; sometimes, the protagonist and antagonist can be viewed as foils for one another.

Genre: a category of narrative which is defined by shared and distinct conventions which arises through repeated usage of those conventions.

Goal: a condition of a game which needs to be met in order to advance to a further stage, and, ultimately, win the game.

Graphic novel: a spine-bound book of comics content that is in and of itself a complete work.

Hyperlink adventure: an interactive, text-based narrative which is navigated through clicking on hyperlinks to be taken to different digital locations.

Intent, reception, and effect (IRE): a paradigm for understanding works in relation to the creator's intent, to how the audience received the work, or to the greater effect the work had beyond its creator and audience.

Mechanics: the base-level actions a player can take when in a structured interactive environment.

Medium: a method with unique properties for disseminating information which differentiate it from other media *and* which is indivisible from the information it is disseminating.

Motif: a recurring symbol or concept which is shown to the audience and which helps develop one or more of the work's themes.

Music: the patterned employment of sound waves to deliver a sensory experience to a receiver which is not solely based in words.

Novel: an extended, complete work of prose fiction, able to be split up into many individual sections of story and capable of focusing on a large or small set of characters, themes, or other narrative elements equally adeptly.

Novelette: a complete work of prose fiction which focuses on more than a singular experience, and which can be broken into at least two smaller, roughly equal sections of narrative.

Novella: a complete work of prose fiction which focuses on more than a singular experience and which can be broken up into at least four smaller, roughly equal sections of narrative.

Philosophical dialogue: a discussion between two or more characters about one or more ideas, written in the form of a script, in which the

intent is to come to some conclusion about the ideas through the
discussion.

Platform: a physical or digital space upon which a medium is dependent to
acted on stage as a theatrical production.

Play script: a text written in the form of a script with the intent for it to be
acted on stage as a theatrical production.

Plot utility character: a character whose sole purpose is to advance the
plot, and has no purpose beyond that (ex. redshirts in *Star Trek* media).

Podcast: a digital recording of audio which is posted online for receivers to
listen to whenever they please.

Poetry: written, spoken, or signed work with the first focus on the language
itself, rather than the information the language conveys.

Prose: any narrative writing whose primary focus is on neither poetic
expression nor instructions for a theoretical experience in a medium
other than the written one.

Protagonist(s): the focal character or characters, the one whose point(s)-of-
view we'll be following in the story.

Protagonist-centered morality: a concept that says that audience
identification with a protagonist is a more powerful determiner of the
audience's allegiance to the protagonist than any actions that the
protagonist takes.

Queer coding: connoting that characters are gay, lesbian, bisexual, transgender, etc. through coding (see "Coding" definition).

Radio: a medium wherein which sound waves transmit information widely, to individual receivers simultaneously.

Screenplay: a script written as a set of instructions for the creation of a film.

Script: a set of instructions for a theoretical experience in a medium other than the written one.

Seasonal anthology: a television show where the cast and story change every season (or "series," the non-American term for a TV season).

Sequential art: a sequence of images used to tell a narrative.

Serial film: a film divided into chapters, each one shown in a theater about every week, like episodes of a television series.

Serialization: the process of dividing a story into several chunks and delivering them piecemeal to the audience.

Setting: the place or places in which a story takes place, defined by physical location, time period, and the restrictions that are placed upon the plot and characters by the place or places.

Short story: a complete work of prose fiction which provides a focused, unified narrative experience to the reader.

Speech prefix: the character names in scripts which precede the lines of dialogue to be spoken by the character indicated by the name.

Standalone story: a story that is a complete work (meaning it has a defined beginning, middle, and end) and stands by itself.

Story: a sequence of intentionally-collected actions and/or events which each change the dynamics of their scene and which also cohere together to convey an experience through a medium to a receiver.

Subgenre: a specialized subcategory of one genre or of a combination of genres. Subgenres can spin out into their own separate genres, if the subgenre is common enough, and specialized enough to distinguish itself from being purely a subcategory of its parent genre(s).

Supporting character: somewhat self-explanatory; a character whose role is to provide support to either the protagonist or the antagonist, while not themselves being a focus. (Ex. love interest, friend, mentor, etc.)

Symbol: a concrete noun, such as a person, a place, a color, an object, etc., used to represent an abstract noun, such as death, chaos, aging, etc.

Teleplay: a script written as a set of instructions for the creation of an episode of a television series.

Television: a sequence of animated or photographic images which create the illusion of motion and whose narratives are both serialized and transmitted to individuals separately.

Text adventure: an interactive, text-based narrative which is navigated through the use of text commands typed through a keyboard into a computer.

Theater: the performance of at least one fictional character by an actor in the same space as the audience.

Theme: an idea which is explored through the story and which becomes core to the understanding of the work by the receiver.

Tone: the story's emotional atmosphere, defined by the emotions which it evokes in its audience.

Tritagonist: a rare term used to describe a tertiary protagonist, one who is even less of a focus than the protagonist(s) and the deuteragonist(s).

Video: a visual medium defined by its ability to allow individuals to create narratives of their own initiative by breaking down the traditional barriers to entry.

Win state: an outcome that happens once certain conditions are satisfied, and which indicates that a player has finished the game with success.

About the Author

Ryan Ten is a graduate of the University of Virginia's Department of Media Studies. While he's been writing fiction since he was ten years old, this is his first book-length nonfiction work, as well as his first published book. When he's not writing, or working on media projects, he's either reading, watching YouTube, listening to podcasts, or at an actual job.

www.ingramcontent.com/pod-product-compliance
Lightning Source LLC
Chambersburg PA
CBHW070328220526
45467CB00001B/69